The Winner's
MIND

CRAIG HADFIELD

COPYRIGHT

This book is copyright. Apart for any fair dealings for private study, research or review, permitted under the Copyright Act 1968, no part of this book may be stored or reproduced without prior written permission from the publisher.

Copyright © Craig Hadfield 2012

Published by Craig Hadfield
www.craighadfield.com.au
Email: craig@craighadfield.com.au

First published in 2012

Book layout and cover design
Publicious P/L
www.publicious.com.au

Cover image © freshidea - Fotolia.com

Cataloguing-in-Publication details on request

Author: Craig Hadfield
Title: The Winner's Mind
ISBN: 978-0-9874384-0-9

Also available as an ebook
ebook ISBN: 978-0-9874384-1-6

To you the reader…for taking the time to never stop learning

CONTENTS

ACKNOWLEDGEMENTS
FOREWORD

PART 1

1. WHERE IT ALL BEGAN 1

The coaching journey
My four BIG lessons
- Lesson 1 – It's not easy
- Lesson 2 – We learn from what we don't do
- Lesson 3 – The power of acknowledgement
- Lesson 4 – Speaking the unsaid

Applying coaching to real estate
What is coaching REALLY?

2. HABITS – THE GOOD and the BAD 19

High performers just do it differently
The habits ALL high performers possess
- Habit 1 – Constant learning and practice
- Habit 2 – They think differently
- Habit 3 – Incredible discipline
- Habit 4 – Down time

Change your thinking, change your life
Four simple steps to creating new positive habits
- Step 1 – What is the new habit you want to create?
- Step 2 – You must be willing to change
- Step 3 – Understanding the current habit's impact
- Step 4 – Creating actions to form the new habit

Nurturing the new habit
The training trap

3. BIG BOLD JUICY GOALS 53

The importance of goals
Top three mistakes when setting goals
How goals improve productivity and performance
What are goals?
Goals are not Key Performance Indicators
The four easy steps to creating great goals
Breaking it down
Crafting simple actions
Celebrate

4. INCREDIBLE PRODUCTIVITY 82

Your physical health
Your physical environment
Mental preparation

5. THE PEOPLE THAT MATTER 103

You are the sum of whom you hang with
Getting your friends and family onboard
Surround yourself with high performers
Who's holding you back?

6. REAL ESTATE WITH THE BRAIN IN MIND....110

Prospecting
- Problem 1 – Fear
- Problem 2 – Lack of planning
- Problem 3 – Lack of commitment

7. HIGH PERFORMANCE TEAMS 120

Groups versus teams
6 principles of working with teams
- Setting the stage
- Building a common goal
- Let them do the thinking
- Focus on solutions
- Make them stretch
- Give positive feedback

PART 2 ....**131**

THE PERFECT DAY

This is Chris's story. A high performing agent, he has learnt what it takes to be at the top of his game. He is guided by his habits; however, his habits are those of the elite few. In the second part of this book, I invite you to follow Chris through his day and observe what he does to be one of the best agents imaginable. You will learn what is going on in his brain that is different to other agents – and how you can apply his knowledge and habits to accelerate and enhance your career immediately.

ACKNOWLEDGEMENTS

I feel incredibly blessed to have some amazing people in my life and to have met so many that have had such a profound influence on who I am today. However, one of the greatest lessons from this is that if you not willing to let new people into your life, very little will change. I was raised by my parents to believe that anything is possible and academia is not necessarily the only way to go. They taught me that there is no right or wrong way but to rely on my own instincts to follow my dreams.

To my former boss Scott Baxter, who gave me the chance to pursue finally a career I loved, selling houses. His guidance, incredible insights and support have never wavered throughout my career. His ability to be at the cutting edge of the industry allowed me to become successful within my own business. Without this start, I may be still searching for my passions in life.

To my coaches Gerry Groom and Kerrie Phipps, who have pushed me beyond my own thinking. Gerry is an incredible friend whom has always been my accountability partner and never allowed me to take short cuts in work or life. Never judging or being critical, but always supportive yet challenging, Gerry has pushed me beyond even my own possibilities. Also to Kerrie Phipps, an amazing coach and author. Kerrie's knowledge as an author coupled with her coaching process made this book possible. Having Kerrie to share the joys and many frustrations when writing was invaluable and she played a massive part in my getting this book written.

To Rob, owner of Zest café who allowed me to sit for hours writing while they cleaned up around me long after closing. And all the regulars who cheered me on as they caught me in front of my laptop, day in day out.

I'd also like to thank my mate Josh Phegan, a real estate coach, who inspired me to share what I believe was important with the real estate industry and for taking time to provide feedback along the way. His work ethic and discipline are second to none, recreating a new way, fresh way to sell real estate.

Aunty Veronica was kind enough to proofread the book in record time during her holidays and provided an alternative insight from her years in the corporate world.

And to my family, my wife Geraldine, and kids Lucy and Jake for allowing me to chase my passion for coaching, and for sharing this wonderful journey with me. They have always kept me grounded, knowing what is really important in life. I love you all so much, you are part of everything I am.

FOREWORD

The Winner's Mind is relevant to all potential 'winners', regardless of the area of interest of the 'high achiever'.

From the first day I met Craig, I knew I was dealing with a passionate and successful young man. I am delighted he has taken the time to share his journey with us.

The skills Craig speaks of must be practiced to reach goals and wear the winner's hat. In my experience with great achievers in the music and entertainment industries, the essential ingredients of talent matched with discipline, determination, hard work and a network will make dreams come true.

What I've learned over so many years is that talent is not enough. Craig has analysed the winner's mind because he wants to help highly talented people find the satisfaction in life that he, at such a young age, is experiencing.

My advice to aspiring young performers is follow your dreams and never, ever give up. Apply the principles in this book and you too can make your dreams come true.

Mary Lopez AM
Hon DLitt (UWS), FFCSME, B.Mus.Ed, DSME, A.Mus.A
Entertainment and Talent Director
TDP Artistic Director and CEO
Emeritus Director Schools Spectacular

1

WHERE IT ALL BEGAN

*"Life isn't about finding yourself.
Life is about creating yourself."*
– George Bernard Shaw

These past ten years, I've attended countless sales seminars, workshops and training events. On the whole, I've always managed to get some great ideas that have helped me keep focused on what needs to be done to be the best real estate agent possible. Many of the lessons I've learnt have been implemented into my business and career and have been pivotal to my success. As time went on, I began to realise that much of the content was the same; the lessons being taught were simply redressed in different clothes. The trainer looked different but the message was pretty much the same. Post training, I found that the conversation was often "That was great, wasn't she a wonderful speaker, but I've heard a lot of that before". And "I really need to start doing that" or "I heard that a year ago" and "I used to do that, I just keep getting too busy."

I found myself saying these same things to myself or to others, which really started to get me thinking "Why don't we do what we know we should?" It wasn't until I started my training as a coach that I began to find the answers.

I remember attending one of the huge training events where a well-known guru in the industry was asked why he is so willing to share his tips and ideas with thousands of other agents. Won't they use this against him? "No," he replied. "What I know is that less than twenty per cent of the people in this room will implement anything of what is learnt and even less will continue on with the new learning consistently."

What he was saying is that most agents have the knowledge but very few implement what they know. Training is critical in learning and growing and, without training, we couldn't become better. The fact that there are so little done around teaching people how to do what they already know is testament to the fact there are so many trainers teaching the same thing. If we all did what we know we should, many trainers wouldn't exist. I'm not suggesting that there aren't new things to learn and that attending training is not valuable – in fact, it is critical – without it, I wouldn't be writing this book. I'm simply pointing out that training alone is not enough.

Change is hard. This is why we often get drawn to the latest seminar or workshop that promises the one thing that will make all the difference. We will always go for the quickest, simplest solution. The problem is, is that in most cases, a great deal of effort will be needed. This is why most people don't change. It's uncomfortable, it pushes our beliefs and it challenges our existing habits. We are programmed to resist change; it goes right back to our survival instincts. In short, change is hard, sometimes very hard. But this is where the new learning is, this is where life changing moments come from. This is where you need to go if you want long-lasting, positive change in your career. There is no silver bullet, no quick fix but instead a series of small behavioural changes one after the other.

In this book, I'm going to combine my experience in real estate with my abilities as a coach. As a coach, I help others create positive change. It's about knowing what is going on in the brain when we go about our daily routine. As an agent, I will help you understand what is holding you back, how to get more of what you want. It was when I began training as a coach and understanding the neuroscience behind what we do that the big 'Aha!' moment came for me as an agent. The excitement was so great, I decided to write about it in this book. For me, this is the missing link with agents that have great knowledge and skill but still find it hard to gain traction.

Observing some of the great agents around the country, you can quickly see the habits they have that have made them successful. It is not about complicated, fancy ideas but the basics of what most agents already know. The difference is that they are doing what they know they need to do. Their mind set is different, they have formed the habits that led them to success. It's not that they are better skilled, have different knowledge, have access to some special key that others don't, it is simply that they *apply* the knowledge. They are consistent in what is successful for them. They don't deviate from their success path. They have hard wired (unknowingly) the habits they need to be successful.

This book is about the how to *create* the winning habits; not just what the habits are, there is much written about that already. It's about understanding why we don't do what we know we should. It's about knowing that the power of an idea is in the *doing* and in this book, I will show you how to grow the new habits that will support what you already know but are not doing, and how to implement any new ideas and create habits around them. New ideas and habits will no longer drift off into the sunset until you discover them again in training years later.

As coaches, we want to get our clients thinking for themselves; my goal for this book is to get you to create positive change, not just give you more knowledge that won't be used. As you read the book, I encourage you to get into action straight away. Use the area in the back of the book to write down the 'Aha!' moments you have as you read. Write down the things that you want to change. Be active and proactive in your reading.

The skills you learn in this book can be applied not only in real estate but also in all parts of your life. To create change we must form new habits. We need to work out what it is we want and craft a plan to get there. Applying the ideas in this book can transform other parts of your life that you want to change. Whether it's friendships, travel, marriage, relationships with your children or learning to recognise what needs to change, creating the future and working towards that is what this book is all about.

In this book, I share a lot of the ideas and insights that I learned along the way on my journey to becoming a high performing real estate agent, however, I'd love to hear about your journey and what you've learnt from this book that you're putting into practice. Whether it's personal or professional, please share your observations and journey with me. You can find me at www.craighadfield.com.au or email me at craig@craighadfield.com.au

I wish you the very best and look forward to hearing from you,

Regards,

Craig Hadfield, author, speaker, coach

The coaching journey

During my years as an agent, I've had the privilege of meeting many amazing people. People who have such interesting careers and jobs you never thought existed. It's the thing I love most about real estate, the amazing people you meet. Like Mary Lopez. Mary bought and sold with me and during this time, we became great friends. Mary is a very successful business woman who created the largest public schools event in the world, the renowned Schools Spectacular.

Then there was Max. Max was a fairly gruff guy who spoke his mind. We looked after a house he owned in the area and rented it out for him from time to time. After several meetings, my curiosity about knowing what he did grew until, one day, I was at his home and asked him just that. He reached across the table to grab a folder. The front cover showed a picture of a massive drilling rig in some remote bush location. Max was a gold miner. His company explored and drilled for gold. He shared fascinating insights with me as the day went on and I loved every minute of hearing about his journey to his current position.

Gerry also springs to mind. Gerry contacted me about some homes for sale. During these exchanges, I noticed his title at the bottom of his emails, Executive Coach. This caught my attention as I was greatly interested in coaching and training. By this time, I had attended many training events and workshops and thought, one day, I would love to be able to help others with their personal journeys.

During one of our property conversations, I asked Gerry to explain to me what an Executive Coach was. My excitement grew as the conversation went on. I was standing in my back yard on a summer afternoon. It was a day I remember very clearly.

Gerry joined IBM 30 years prior and worked as a senior sales executive throughout the world, coaching internal team members in sales. A passion to grow his team became his primary focus as he recognised that through coaching he could have an influence on their thinking, which would then create a winning mindset throughout the company. Gerry successfully won many multimillion dollar contracts during his years at IBM and developed one of the most dynamic and high performance sales teams in the organisation. After so many amazing years with IBM, Gerry felt a need to spread his knowledge further; he wanted to take his incredible coaching skills beyond the boundaries of the company. After a great deal of deliberation, he formally resigned to pursue his passion in coaching. Understanding what a loss Gerry was to the company, IBM encouraged him to continue on as a coach working with key people within the business in a consultancy role. Gerry continues to work with IBM today.

Gerry's passion to help others was incredibly inspiring and, for the first time in my life, I felt that I may have found my passion. The ability to use my skills in work and life to help others grow was very exciting. I think many people want to experience the feeling you get when you make a difference in other people's lives, and I could see this could be it for me.

I have always been a believer that to be able to help someone truly, having had similar experiences allows you to understand at a different level. Knowing this, my first instinct was to get Gerry to coach me, so I could experience what it was like to be coached. Although I had no idea what I was in for, there was a sense of great excitement. It was the first time for a long time that I had put myself in an uncomfortable place. Later, I would learn that this feeling of being uncomfortable is the point where things begin to change. It's the place where most people stop and retract into a place of comfort and safety. However, if we want to bring new and exciting experiences into our lives, we must accept the fact that we need to get a little bit uncomfortable. The lessons I learnt during my time as a coachee were invaluable and today they continue to support my clients through their own personal journey.

My four BIG lessons

Lesson 1 – It's not easy

After meeting Gerry for a general chat, I engaged him for three months of coaching. We went through the process of establishing three inspiring and exciting goals in different areas of my life.

At the time, many changes were happening in the world of real estate because of the global financial crisis, moving offices and changing staff. I was also moving house. Busy kids and all that stuff that life brings were taking up my time. Many days I felt that the coaching was great and other days I felt it was an inconvenience, getting in the way and a waste of time and money, but I persisted. Gerry helped me set small actions that moved me towards my goals. These small actions needed to be completed before the next session. What seemed to be such a simple thing started to become quite difficult. I felt the need to get things done right and, in doing so, sometimes didn't complete on the actions because I was trying to perfect them. Through Gerry's encouragement, I battled on and we shared all the little wins. This was my first understanding that *creating change is hard*. Later when I studied coaching, I would learn why we resist change even though we want it. Understanding what goes on in our brains helped me understand why we do what we do and how we can use that to our advantage.

Lesson 2 – We learn from what we don't do

As we worked through the actions leading towards the goals, there were certain areas that I found very easy and, of course, they were done first. Then there where actions we set that I seemed to keep putting off. At the time, I just convinced myself that I would do them later. However, as time went on, Gerry would draw my attention to the things that weren't getting done. There were many conversations around the actions that I avoided or wouldn't do to my full capacity. Learning to notice these areas made me realise that either I was avoiding the task because it put me in an uncomfortable position or I didn't want what I thought I did. So how do you work out which one it is?

The answer is by setting goals. When going through the goal setting process, you begin to draw your attention to what's important for you or the team. At the end of the process, you should be left with goals that are exciting and inspiring. It's like sifting for gold and the more you sift, the more gold starts to show up. Of course there are also times when you begin to work towards a goal to discover that areas stand out that are no longer important. The goal you developed may be something you've always dreamed of but as you work though the actions and begin to notice what's not getting done, you will start to realise that the goal may not be what you really wanted. This may sound strange, however it's very common for many people. We often dream of things but on a subconscious level, know it's not something we will ever do. But we convince ourselves that it's okay to dream. And it is. However, too much dreaming can get in the way of creating real, positive and exciting change. Or you may find that your goal is not as high on the to-do list as you first thought. Clarifying what goals are important will help you rearrange your priorities.

Often when I work with people around work or career related goals, they are resistant to spend time in their personal area. In most cases, however, this changes as they work through their goals. At some point, the client realises the importance of life outside of work and the focus starts to shift in another direction. What they first thought they wanted (career advancement, more money, etc) is replaced with happiness, better relationships with family and friends and so on. This became very true for me in my journey as a coachee with Gerry, and completely changed my life.

However, perhaps your goal is not something you want right now. The exciting part of this is the sense of freedom it gives you. To have something burning on your mind for days, weeks or perhaps years and to only then discover that it's not that important is like a massive weight lifting from your shoulders. It creates space to work on other areas that are more relevant and exciting for you now. Learning to know what you don't want is just as powerful as knowing what you do want.

Lesson 3 – The power of acknowledgement

The power of acknowledgement was and still remains the greatest lesson of all and something that I use every day in and out of coaching. We were discussing some business challenges in a session one day and we talked about why it is we employ people. And like most employers, the answer seemed obvious, to fill a certain role. Of course, that answer was too simple. Gerry challenged me to think hard about the characteristics, values and skills that made me choose one person over another when interviewing them for the first time. We went on to discuss each team member and what was great about them as people and work colleagues. At that point, I was reminded of all the great things they do day-to-day when there is a tendency to look for what is going wrong day-to-day. I thought that they knew how I felt, but It was clear I hadn't made the effort to speak it out loud. We began with meeting and talking about what was going well, and encouraging each other to acknowledge something that was positive about one another. I would later learn when becoming a coach that in order for people to create new positive habits, they need lots of genuine encouragement and acknowledgement. It's this constant feedback that supports and reinforces the new thinking of the new habit.

The best way to understand this is the metaphor or when you get a new pet. We encourage them to do new tricks with lots of rewards and encouragement. As time goes on, the trick becomes second nature and less encouragement is needed. The same applies for humans. We must nurture new habits, particularly in the early stages. This is when people are most vulnerable. Gerry went on to ask me to find someone to acknowledge every day. I thought it was going to be easy, but it was one of the hardest things I had to do. I persisted as the amazing response from the often surprised recipient encouraged me to keep going. This lesson in acknowledgement showed what power acknowledgement added to my relationships with others. The consistency of me having to do it day in day out helped me form acknowledgement as a powerful new habit. What was once very hard I now I find easy and take great pleasure in doing, particularly watching the smiles it puts on people's faces.

Lesson 4 – Speaking the unsaid

When I began being coached, I didn't share my experience with anyone at first. I was afraid that people would find it a bit weird, or friends would think that I was hitting my mid life crisis early. I developed a story in my head as to how people would perceive it. Of course, Gerry encouraged me to start to share what I was doing. I remember sitting with a friend, Phil, at a local coffee shop and we started talking about what was going on in our lives. Suddenly, I started to think of what I had been talking to Gerry about. As I was having this conversation with Phil, I started the self-talk, encouraging myself to share the fact I was coached. It was an amazing feeling to know you're about to say something that can't be taken back. My stomach was churning, I was getting sweaty palms but decided to go for it anyway. Well, the reaction was nothing like I expected. Phil was intrigued and started asking all sorts of questions about what it was, how it worked and so on. But the thing that surprised me most was that he thought it was such a fantastic idea!

At that moment, I learnt that most often the story we create is far from the reality and that speaking what's unsaid can be incredibly powerful. I often share this story in coaching when people are afraid to say what they really think for fear that something bad may come of it. As a result of me speaking the unsaid, I felt a massive weight lift and it opened a door to move my relationship with Phil to a new level. Suddenly, there was more to talk about and over time he began sharing things with me on a personal level, which was a result of building trust by not being afraid of saying things that may make you feel uncomfortable.

During my coaching journey, I became more and more interested in becoming a coach. Having experienced that power of helping people move in a positive direction was something I wanted to share with others. So I began studying coaching with Results Coaching, a coaching organisation developed on the latest neuroscience research.

During the next two years, I would continue to coach and train, expanding my knowledge and experience into coaching teams and team leaders.

During this time, I also continued to run my own real estate offices and started to recognise areas that with coaching, could dramatically improve individual and team performances. Even though I was involved in training real estate agents, I began to introduce coaching I had learnt with great results. There was a dramatic improvement in engagement with agents and teams. There was a greater sense of enthusiasm and desire to learn. This was the point when I realised that it was coaching in the critical habits that was the missing link to success.

Applying coaching to real estate

As I studied coaching, I learnt the power it can have to changing people's lives and the great satisfaction to be gained from helping people discover what they want and how to get there. As a real estate agent, I reflected on how coaching could apply to my industry. There were many trainers in the market teaching skills, scripts and dialogues and many successful agents talking about how they got to where they are now.

One of the biggest issues in the real estate industry is not the lack of knowledge, information, systems or technology. That's everywhere and easily accessible. The problem for agents and managers is *getting done what needs to be done.* As a coach, I could clearly see what was missing from our industry when it came to training. No one was teaching agents how to create the positive habits needed to be successful. We could learn what those habits were, but very little was spoken about how to create the habits.

This is the missing link for agents. Most agents are well-meaning and are well-trained or have access to great training. So why do eighty per cent of all agents perform below average? The key is to understand how our brains work and how to use that knowledge to our advantage. Understanding what agents go through every day, I could see where things were going wrong. Equally, when I listen to top performers, they were instinctively doing the things that support the right thinking. They had unknowingly worked out how to use their brain to apply the habits that made them a top performer.

So I began on a different path, teaching agents how to create the top performing habits. My goal was to help them to become *aware* of their thinking and to then *think for themselves.* This is because coaches know that if a coachee can think for themselves, their new ideas and habits are more likely to stick. I began teaching agents how to create new habits that will serve them over and over without relying on short chunks of motivational talks to keep them on track. My job as a coach is to get people thinking for themselves, to stretch their thinking beyond their current mindset. Teaching this thinking to agents is the missing link in consistency around the positive habits they need to become successful. Showing owners and managers how to support the new habits in meetings and conversations within their business is another role as coach. After all, if the new habits aren't encouraged and nurtured, they can't be developed.

There are many great trainers that call themselves coaches. It's important to understand what the difference is. Trainers play a vital role in the development of agents. They provide the knowledge they need to become great performers. The industry is forever changing and continuous training is needed. New ideas and technology are constantly hitting the market and trainers play a vital role in teaching agents what they need to know. We need to know what to say and when to say it. We need to learn how to win business and sell and, without training, it's not possible to perform at our optimum. Training is about acquiring skills.

What coaching REALLY is

Coaching differs in several areas. The key difference is that, in coaching, the participants do most of the thinking. As a coach, I want to facilitate positive change through improved thinking. I want the clients to do most of the thinking themselves. This will give the participants the best chance to develop new thinking for themselves. This new thinking is much more likely to be sustained.

Coaching is not training. A trainer will present areas of learning for the participants. There is a set outcome and usually specific outcomes for the participants. Where coaching differs is that the coachees or participants drive the agenda with the focus around working towards a specific set of goals. Coaching is about changing behaviour.

In real estate, trainers provide the what to do, but often fail to deliver the how and why to do it. For example, a trainer may suggest that to build a great career in real estate, you need to be an active prospector, and this is very true. The greatest agents are the greatest prospectors. This may include many different ways of generating leads such as calling past appraisals. So the trainer will suggest that the participant make a certain number of calls over a certain number of days etc. The trainer will also suggest when they make these calls, what to say and so on. The problem is that most agents already know this but they are not doing it. And this is usually when the training stops.

There are many frustrated agents and business owners who have great intentions but lack constancy around these critical habits. To become a high performer, these are the actions that must be done, no matter what level you are at. For a new agent into the industry, these are the habits that will ensure they have a long and prosperous career in real estate. These are the habits agents who have been in the industry for longer already know they should have under their belt to be a high performer.

By bringing my experience as an agent together with becoming a coach, I realised that the approach to learning needed to change.

The diagram on the next page explains the difference between different styles of approach when working with people. All styles are used in the context of trying to help others, however, as a coach, we rarely go into the other quadrants.

Therapy and counselling are left to trained professionals. I'm far from an expert in this area, however, their style will be in part about asking questions to get to the heart of the problem.

In the area of *management,* there is a tendency to focus on telling others about problems or what is not going well.

Trainers are there to provide answers and to develop skills and knowledge around certain areas. A coach will from time to time move into this area, particularly if they are an expert in the field they are coaching. However, the trainer spends most of their time telling others what to do in order to give them the skills and knowledge required.

Coaching is about helping others find their own solutions though a series of questions. There is a basic assertion that the coachee has the answers within and, with the right questions, the answers will eventually come. Coaching acts on the basic premise that if the coachee finds their own solutions, the solution is much more likely to 'stick'.

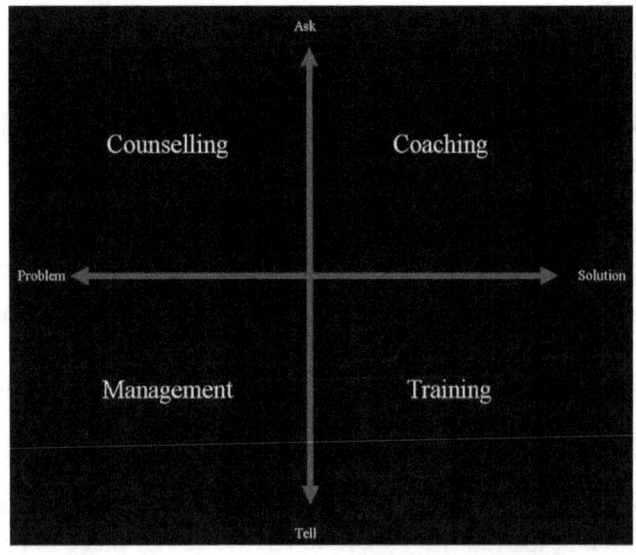

Adapted from Results Coaching manual

2

HABITS – THE GOOD and the BAD

"No need to focus on the fruits of your action but the action itself."

High performers just do it differently

High performers do what they know they should. This seems fairly obvious, however, getting someone to do what is required is very difficult. Why? Real estate agents are human too. They will do what comes easy, resist change and have a natural tendency towards fear. It's a natural human instinct to resist change as it's part of our evolution to survive. Our brains are set up in a slight state of fear for the same reason. We are in a natural state of fear as part of our protection and survival mechanism and it's our default mental state. This is why when we enter a room full of strangers, we can suffer uncertainty and anxiousness.

Often we develop habits around the resistance to change and fear and, as those habits are embedded deeper into our brains, it becomes more and more difficult to change.

It's very easy for an agent to be busy from day-to-day and be highly unproductive. I determine productivity in real estate agents by carrying out dollar productive tasks. This means performing those tasks that lead to current and future business. Within any given day, you can be out with buyers, calling solicitors, making prospecting calls, talking with past clients, arranging pest and building reports, as well as having sales meetings and training staff. These are just some of the many action items required of any agent on a daily basis.

These tasks can make an agent very busy, but many of them don't lead to future or current business. Future business is generated from identifying future sellers and building a relationship of trust until they are ready to sell. The challenge with real estate is that it requires endurance. It can take weeks, months and often years to connect, develop the trust and move the client to a position where they are ready to sell. Industry statistics suggest it can take from between three months and three years from the time you meet a potential seller to the time they go to market. This process takes a certain amount of skill, but it mostly takes discipline. It takes discipline to be consistent around the activities that will lead the client forward, while developing trust at the same time.

High performers spend the majority of their time in the area of looking for and nurturing future business. They display the disciplines of regular contact with numerous potential clients via multiple contact points, thus allowing trust to develop over time. In the future, when the seller is ready to sell, the high performer has been so consistent around the trust building behaviours, (ie. calling, face to face contact, letters, emailing etc), that the seller will at the very least allow them to be considered when it comes time to sell. Most often, however, they have been so consistent with their contact, the seller will only choose them, leading to a higher appraisal to list ratio and higher average fee.

Often, new agents wonder what secrets the high performers have? What training do they have that has led to their success? The reality is that they possess laser-like focus on doing what needs to be done. They won't allow distractions, they set a path and won't deviate. They may use multiple mediums to prospect, however, there is always consistency in when and how they do it.

It's common for a new sales person with good training to outperform someone with many more years of experience. Providing that their physical and mental space is supported around these discipline habits, they can build their future business very quickly. The more experienced agent can often, to their peril, fall back on their skills and history to try and get by. They can also fall into the success trap and suddenly stop doing what made them successful in the past. This is where real estate agents can experience the roller-coaster of sales – the typical cycle of boom then bust. When faced with a shortage of listings, the typical agent will go back to what is needed to find more business. They begin to work, often still inconsistently, in dollar productive activities. They continue to do this until they have something to sell, then get busy selling. During this phase, they again slow down or stop dollar productive activities that generate future business because they get busy selling. The money starts to come in from the sales and then they do even less, again beginning to relax and feel more comfortable. Then as the sales dry up, they wait until crisis point with nothing to sell and start dollar productivities again, and so the cycle begins again.

There is no doubt that good training, sales experience and years on the job give the seasoned real estate agent an advantage. However, without the discipline of performing high dollar activities, they too will suffer and look to blame outside influences for their failures. They will be the most likely to go through the boom to bust selling cycle.

Seasoned agents can also suffer from the success delusion as well. The success delusion is when you believe that what got you here in the first place will be enough to get you to the next. Often, successful agents trying to grow have more difficulty changing because they feel that if they do more of the same, it will grow their business. This is true to an extent. They need to continue to do what works. However, successful real estate agents still have blockages.

As a coach, average to good agents are often the most difficult to grow because of their strong belief in their success to date. They can be found at times finding blame outside themselves as to why things aren't growing or going well. We hear it all the time. It's the market, it's interest rates, the rain, the wind. Excuses are everywhere. Compounding this attitude is their manager or boss's belief and contribution to the success delusion. Managers accept that because their agents have been successful in the past, there must be something else that is creating the blockages. If the managers were to pull apart the non-performing seasoned agent's day like they might with a rookie, they would discover that the same lack of discipline around performing the activities that create the future business is causing the lack of business.

Given that it can take months or even years to generate new business, what activities are done today will be the results in thirty, sixty or ninety days or months down the track. Similarly, what is happening today is the result of what was or wasn't done months ago.

Learning what the success habits are isn't too difficult. Finding a great trainer and attending their seminars and workshops will lead to great knowledge. Watching and listening to high performers and taking note of what they do will give tremendous insights to the habits of highly successful agents.

Understanding what it is they do is the first step in creating long-lasting critical habits of successful real estate. You must first know what to do before you can learn how to do it. Once you understand what it is that high performers do, you can move to create the habits that will be sustainable for you and will lead to success.

The habits ALL high performers possess

Habit 1 – Constant learning and practice

High performing agents acknowledge that they need to stay at the cutting edge of ideas. Whether it's social media, video, scripts and dialogue, they never stop learning. Many high performers spend time coaching and training others, which not only shares their knowledge but also reinforces the habits they already have. This is a form of self-acknowledgement and praise through giving something of themselves. They look and listen to what is going on around them and train to fix the gaps and blockages. They are lifelong learners who accept that there may be a better way of achieving greater results.

They invest both time and money into themselves, understanding that they are their own best investment. They see training and learning not as a cost but as a critical discipline that will lead to results.

Habit 2 – They think differently

Top performing agents have an abundance mindset. They look at the glass as half full, not empty. They know that the business is out there, they just need to hunt it down. Like many sales related jobs, they experience constant rejection from buyers, sellers and sometimes even their peers. The top performer isn't immune to this rejection; in fact, they could possibly receive more rejection as they are talking with more people. However, how they handle this rejection is different. They are true optimists and don't take rejection personally. They accept that it is just a normal part of their job and that they will encounter it most days of their career.

Many agents may see themselves as optimists but a high performer recovers from rejection quicker.

Here are two examples:

Agent A has pitched for some new business and is feeling confident. He has done all the right things and is well-trained around what to say and when. He receives a call to advise he has missed out on the business to a competitor and is not needed. Agent A can't understand why. After all, he did everything right and had built a good rapport with the client. However, the negative thoughts of self-doubt creep in. Agent A starts to question where he went wrong, what he didn't do well and looks to lay blame. This now affects the agent's thinking for the rest of the day or possibly days and sometimes weeks! Agent A will also gather his peers around to get reassurance that what he did was right and he couldn't have done anything else. Agent A looks for support as to why he has failed and starts to believe it was external factors, not himself. He eventually puts it down to the client not wanting to auction or the competition's fee was lower or perhaps even worse still, he didn't want the business anyway, it was going to be too hard to sell!

Agent B gets the same rejection, however, he thinks about things differently. He will have a look at what he may have done differently but focuses on what he did well. Agent B chalks it up to part of his day and moves on to the next sale.

High performing agents simply move on quicker both physically and mentally. They don't allow the distraction of rejection to hold them back. In his book *Learned Optimism,* Martin Seligman demonstrates that the optimism of a person is one of the most critical traits of a high producing sales person. This ability to not take rejection personally and move on quickly allows time to get to the next sale. A high performer knows that just because they may have not won this time, it has no bearing on the next deal. They know that the sales are not linked together. Each sale stands on its own. This mindset is the key component to success in a high performer. They control what they think and don't allow negativity to enter their headspace. They can self-acknowledge what is going well and what needs improving. They don't need constant praise because they can praise themselves. Taking the time to self-acknowledge further develops the high performing critical habit of moving on quickly. The high performer can self-diagnose and doesn't look to others to critique them. They will happily listen to impartial feedback and allow themselves to be open to new learning that will plug any holes in their processes.

Habit 3 – Incredible discipline

Discipline is probably the most important attribute of a high performing agent. They understand that, without discipline, all the training and practice in the world will be of little use. They know what it is they need to do, day in day out, and they don't deviate from that path. They prepare for chaos but because they have done all the high dollar productive work consistently, this becomes only a small distraction and then they are quickly back on track. They have laser-like focus around what is important to get done in the coming days and weeks. They have a very clear idea, usually in the form of well-crafted goals that they must drive towards.

High performers know their physical and mental capabilities well. They listen to their bodies and know how their energy works best. They get the productive activities done first, and leave all the low level thinking like emails and reports to last. They make others work around their ideal schedule and not the other way around. They prepare and plan constantly so they hit the ground running. They know exactly what they are going to do every day before they start.

They operate with the same discipline outside of work as in. They understand that keeping a healthy mind requires a healthy body. They have a regular routine of eating and exercise that they stick with. They aren't necessarily marathon runners or triathletes, they are just consistent around being healthy for the most part. This is not to say they don't enjoy certain indulgences, in fact, they know the importance of rewards after effort. However, their wellbeing is the overriding habit that they support.

Habit 4 – Down time

A high performing agent understands that to perform at one hundred per cent when working, they need sufficient down time. They value that their time off is as important as their time on. They understand that to be able to think at a high level with great energy, they need down time to recover. They see themselves like high performing athletes that can only perform at the top and they allow time to rest. They take time out to pursue other interests that are separate to real estate. They have social circles that extend outside their career, which helps provide balance and relaxes their minds.

High performers plan well in advance for their breaks and won't allow for distractions during this time. High performers know that their best thinking is often done when they are away from the pressures of work. We are constantly surrounded by information with applications such as Facebook, iPhones, Blackberries and Twitter, just to name a few. A high performer understands that to switch off, they also need to switch off the input from all these channels. Resting the mind is even more important than resting the body. An elite bodybuilder or weightlifter plans their rest time as this is when the muscles recover from damage and new muscle fibres grow. The same can be said for our mental state. Real estate is a high level thinking career and we cannot sustain high level thinking week in week out. A high performer has several short breaks, this may be regular weekends or short weeks where they leave the real estate space altogether. On top of this, they plan a minimum of six to eight longer breaks throughout the year. They set up systems and procedures that support them while they are off so their down time isn't disturbed.

My Top 5 Lessons

1. **Watch and learn from highly successful agents**

2. **Never think you have nothing new to learn**

3. **Think like a high performer**

4. **The predominant habit is consistency and discipline**

5. **Balance hard work with quality time off**

Change your thinking, change your life

I'm a naturally anxious person and have struggled over the years with negative thinking. During the course of owning my own business, we suffered many setbacks and financial pressures that would lead to negative thinking. This could sometimes go on for days or weeks at a time. I did however recognise this thinking and worked extremely hard on trying to control these thoughts as I knew they were a distraction from everything I wanted to achieve. It not only affected my work life, it also flowed through into my personal life, meaning I became disconnected from family and friends. I knew that I wasn't always present but I couldn't see a way through it. I was waiting for something to change and of course it never did. I had to learn to change myself.

Being coached was the first step in becoming more aware of what was going on for me. I would learn over time and, through becoming a coach, becoming mindful was the first step to creating change. It seems so obvious now that changing the way you think will change the way you feel, but it took a while to finally click for me. I'm not a spiritual person but certainly find people's faith very interesting, particularly as a coach. To see others so focused on something higher such as God or Buddha brings me back to the importance of focusing on something higher than what's going on day-to-day. Goals can work in a similar way. I don't see mindfulness as restricted to people who meditate or pray, but I certainly do value the ability to become aware of what's going on around you while being focused and 'present' or 'in the moment'. For me, it's about thinking about your thinking.

Another great way to understand mindfulness is to think of what the opposite is, mindlessness. We hear people talking about doing mindless acts, whereby whatever the action, no thought has entered into it. They act without thinking and suffer the consequences of their actions.

Becoming mindful is critical to creating change; after all, our thoughts control our feelings, which impact our actions. In the sporting arena, evidence abounds to suggest that it is an athlete's ability to control their mind that separates the good from the great. No matter how much training they do, how well they eat and rest, if their mind is not focused on the task at hand, they will come off second best.

A great example of this is a basketball player. For part of the game, the pace is fast and aggressive and requires quick, instinctive action. The player needs to make split second decisions as to where to pass and where to move. Then, within seconds, they could be faced with having to make a penalty shot. They now need to change their focus to calm and still, to shoot the penalty accurately. This requires a huge shift in thought in a split second. They need to settle both physically and mentally to get ready to shoot. Over time, the amount of mindfulness required will become less as habits are created through practice, but mindfulness will prevail.

The same applies to real estate agents. Regardless of all the planning that can be in place things happen that will affect our state of mind. Both positive and negative inputs are all around us and it is how we react to these inputs that will ultimately determine our overall performance day-to-day and week-to-week.

As well as distractions, as sales people, our mindset is critical to our performance. If we enter the sales process looking for new business without the right thinking, we are likely to fail or fall well short of what we want and expect from ourselves. The more we prepare mentally for distractions, chaos, the unexpected, rejection and so on, the better we will be equipped at handling the situation. The faster we can refocus our thinking, the faster we can get on with what's important to staying highly productive. If we begin with a negative mindset, it is harder to recover. Unexpected interruptions good and bad will seem far worse than reality and our recovery rate will be much slower.

In his book *Your Brain at Work,* David Rock talks about the natural state of being for our minds and how it affects productivity. He says that, as humans, we are either in a state of Toward or Away, meaning our brains are in a state of fight or flight. In other words, feeling optimistic or anxious.

AWAY   TOWARDS

This state of mind has a huge bearing on how we get things done and how we react to certain situations. We are naturally born in an away state, meaning our natural tendency is caution or flight. Our natural instincts are to judge every situation and people we don't know as a threat until we see otherwise. This feeling can be so subtle that we are not even conscious of it. Knowing it exists is important in terms of our ability to get things done and create change when it is necessary. Because change is a natural threat and we are already in a state of threat, any activity that challenges what we are currently comfortable with will create a flight instinct. We have a natural tendency to push back. If we want to create change and try new things to move us to a new level, understanding what is going on is critical.

It is also understood that to have good quality, high level thinking such as problem solving, we need to be in this toward mental state. The more anxious we are, the more we react instinctively and our ability to think clearly becomes distorted. We start to go on auto pilot. It is much easier to recover from a setback when we are mentally in a positive or toward state. The other side to this is that if we are already in an away state or negative mental place when something goes wrong, the tendency is to fall deeper and faster into a higher state of anxiousness. Of course, it then becomes much more difficult to move back into a toward state from that higher state of anxiety.

Becoming mindful and recognising that being anxious is a natural reaction to change and that resistance to change is normal, we can start to put into place a plan to deal with these feelings when they arise. We can plan for these reactions early so we are in a toward state mentally or a positive frame of mind, prior to change or chaos that might interrupt our day.

As agents, we are constantly being pulled into a state of chaos with negotiations, inspections reports and deadlines. Knowing how to start every day in a toward state will keep you thinking at a higher level when problems arise.

Your ability to think at a high level during negotiations or listings will be vastly improved. Being in the toward state will buffer you from feelings of rejection when chasing new business and you will recover at a much faster rate, ready to go again.

My Top 5 Lessons

- **You need to become more mindful**
- **Our natural state is towards anxiousness**
- **You need to move to a toward state to think clearly**
- **Move to a toward state as quickly as you can**
- **Being in a toward state will help you keep calm when things go wrong**

> *"We are what we repeatedly do. Excellence, then is not an act, but a habit."*
> – Aristotle

Four simple steps to creating new positive habits

As humans we are driven by habits that have been developed through our years of living. Some we learnt in childhood, some we are born with. Others we developed ourselves through learning and practicing. No matter how they came about, our habits make up for a large part of who we are and what we do.

Kevin Ochsner, Ph.D. is one of the founding fathers of the social neuroscience field and Head of the Social Cognitive Neuroscience Lab at Columbia University. In his research, he found that, conservatively, humans are guided by habits seventy to ninety per cent of the time and by deliberate thought ten to thirty per cent of the time.

This is an important statistic to understand before we begin to learn what is required to create positive, long-lasting change. Creating change and implementing new learning requires creating new habits. It is widely understood through modern neuroscience that old habits can't be changed, new habits need to be formed. What this means is that all the current habits we have are virtually with us forever and will remain hard-wired in our brains. We therefore need to create new ones that become the dominant habit over time. This explains why when we try and create a new habit we often fail, falling back into our existing ways.

If you think about driving to a particular place regularly, say work, the first time we drive there we may have needed a map. Over time, the route becomes familiar and we no longer need to think about how to get to work anymore, it has become a habit. If we then decide to drive a different way, we may need to get the map out again, it will require a lot more thinking. Over time, however, this new way will become normal and less thinking will be required. However, if you decide to go the old way again for a change, it's likely you would remember the way fairly easily. It's stayed in your memory from driving that route day after day.

As you can see, even the most simple change can be difficult at first, so depending on how much change you want, creating new habits can take time and a great deal of effort. Knowing this, there is a process required to create sustainable, long-lasting, positive change. The formula stays the same no matter what it is you want to change. Whether it's work related, personal or social, knowing what is needed to create the new habit is the first step.

Step 1 – What is the new habit you want to create?

Take the time to understand what it is you want to change. This may seem simple but if the habit you want to create is not clear, it is difficult to know what you need to do to change. You also need to come from a positive point of view. For example… Change "I don't want to procrastinate any more" to "I want to launch into action". You are coming from a place of what you want (towards) versus what you don't want (away).

Another way to look at it is asking what is the opposite of the existing habit you want to change?

For example: The current habit is "I currently don't work consistently". The opposite of this or the new habit you want to create could be "I am consistent in my work". This becomes the new habit you want to build. Spend the time to identify what new habit you want to create before moving to the next step.

Step 2 – You must be willing to change

Our habits can go back years and often decades, which makes changing very difficult. It is ultimately who we are and how the world sees us. Knowing this fact is critical to bring about long-lasting change. You must possess a keen willingness to want to change. If you are not one hundred per cent committed to the desired change, it's likely the current habit will dominate and very little will happen. As part of the willingness to change, there must also be acknowledgement that the current habit exists. This is often the hurdle that you need to overcome when you are wanting to change. No matter how much effort, energy and training we offer, if the individual does not acknowledge that a change is needed, no change will occur. Without this acknowledgement, it's unlikely there will be any willingness to change.

As a coach, it's impossible to help create change in someone if they aren't willing to change and particularly if they don't feel they need or want to. The willingness to change applies not only to people looking to prosper but also to highly successful individuals. In his paper *The Success Delusion,* Dr Marshall Goldsmith talks about the challenges in getting highly successful people to change. If you are looking at taking a top performing agent to a super high performer, they too must be willing to change. However, they can be stuck within the success delusion that Goldsmith talks about. Given that they are already very successful, they can believe that they should stay the way they are because they have created success by being who they are. This is certainly true in many ways. They have many of the successful habits needed to achieve results, however, to go to the next level, they too must be committed to creating change.

As you can see, no matter what level you are at, without a willingness to change, new habits can't be formed.

Step 3 – Understanding the current habit's impact

Understanding how our existing habits affect us is a key component in creating a new habit. By fully recognising how existing habits impact on our lives, it brings the habit front and centre and helps identify the need to change. The impact of some habits may seem obvious and the results very clear, whereas other habits may be less obvious and the impact also not so obvious.

An example of a habit that has a big impact may be smoking. The impact of the habit is clear; chances are you will become sick and die and this will no doubt have an impact, certainly on yourself! However, thinking this example through shows that there are many more impacts to this habit. For example, upon your death your family could face financial hardship, which in turn could force the sale of assets, which in turn could affect the quality of your family's livelihood and so on. So you see that a habit that has a dramatic impact such as death can have a further series of impacts that affect others long after you're gone.

However, the same can be said for habits that seem to be less obvious or have a perception of having very little to no impact at all. These habits are often the ones we carry day-to-day that make up who we are. They may be work related or just part of your personality but, either way, these habits good and bad affect what happens around you.

An example of a habit could be that you easily get caught up in office distractions, talking about things that seem very interesting such as what happened on the weekend, how your footy team went or any other normal office conversations. This certainly is a part of our day-to-day work life, however, if it forms a part of a daily or weekly distraction, it can have dramatic consequences.

Let's say you have scheduled to conduct a series of prospecting calls every day for two hours. During this time, you find yourself overhearing and getting involved in other people's conversations. Over the course of the week, due to the distractions, you find yourself falling behind with the number of calls required to hit your targets. The impact of this is that you don't make the required number of calls needed to book the necessary appointments. The impact is that without the required number of appointments booked, the number of homes listed will be below target. The impact of this is that without the number of homes listed for this period, the number of sales falls below your budget. The impact of this is that there is no bonus this quarter. This impact of this is that without the bonus, the family holiday may be in jeopardy. The impact of this creates upset within your family from the disappointment at the prospect that there will be no holiday. The impact of this could go on for some time.

Such a situation can lead to a feeling of disappointment or failure, which can then have a dramatic effect on your mindset. This could in turn affect your work performance even further, and trigger negative self-limited self-talk that can hold you back even further.

Understanding the impact of the negative habits can't be overstated, and you should allow plenty of time to work through the process so you can understand what the full impacts are.

Use the example above as a guide to understand the impact of any negative habits you want to change.

Step 4 – Creating actions to form the new habit

Once you have identified the negative habit you want to change, committed yourself completely to creating a new positive habit and understood the impact of the negative habit, you are ready to start crafting actions to form the new habit.

This is the last but very important step to creating long-lasting change. Once you have identified what habit is holding you back, you need to start to create actions that will lead to creating new habits that will support you for the rest of your life. Given that the old habit you are trying to override may have been with you for a very long time, the actions you take need to be easy and achievable. This is not to say it won't be hard; in fact, it can be very hard. After all, you are trying to create new circuits in your brain to do something completely different or even opposite to what you are used to doing.

When choosing your actions keep them small. Be careful not to group multiple actions together. The more actions you group together, the harder it will become and you may not complete all actions.

Let's say the habit you want to change is "being easily distracted while at work". One of your actions could be to go into a closed office to make your calls. This would be a great action, however it still could be broken down further.

Your action: Go into an office to make your calls

Other actions included in this could be
- Have a meeting with your boss to tell him or her what you are doing and why
- Advise others where you are and that you are not to be disturbed
- Book the office so you are sure you have sole use of the space for the time you need.

Set aside some time to think carefully about any habits that you practice that don't serve you well or limit you in some way. Perhaps focus on one area of your life at a time, such as your career. Once you've decided on a habit that you want to work on and change, write it down below or in your notebook, and then follow the formula above and flesh out the impacts. Next, write down the actions that you plan to take, and the actions that will follow on, to ensure that you now know how to change and adopt a new, more positive habit and a new way of thinking.

HABITS – THE GOOD and the BAD

THE HABIT I WANT TO CHANGE IS:

_____

THE IMPACT OF THIS IS:

_____

THE IMPACT OF THIS IS:

_____

THE IMPACT OF THIS IS:

_____

THE IMPACT OF THIS IS:

_____

THE IMPACT OF THIS IS:

_____

THE IMPACT OF THIS IS:

_____

THE IMPACT OF THIS IS:

THE IMPACT OF THIS IS:

THE IMPACT OF THIS IS:

THE IMPACT OF THIS IS:

ACTION I CAN TAKE:

ACTION I CAN TAKE:

ACTION I CAN TAKE:

HABITS – THE GOOD and the BAD

ACTION I CAN TAKE:

_____

ACTION I CAN TAKE:

_____

ACTION I CAN TAKE:

_____

ACTION I CAN TAKE:

_____

ACTION I CAN TAKE:

_____

Nurturing the new habit

Once you have begun to create the new habits, they must be nurtured to ensure that they grow into long-lasting, sustainable habits. Just like the way we encourage our children through their milestones like their first words and their first steps, we offer huge amounts of encouragement to get them to talk or walk again. Over time, they learn to realise that they get rewarded when they do something positive, which creates new connections around the brain that strengthen the habit over time.

Like with our children, we must reward and encourage ourselves for the new habits we are trying to create. This can be done by self-acknowledgement as well as external acknowledgement. Self-acknowledgement starts by recognising what you have done well yourself. Even if you didn't complete on your actions one hundred per cent, acknowledging what was completed and what went well is critical to the growth of the new habit. If you are working with others or perhaps you have friends or colleagues that are trying to create some new habits, keep a lookout for what they are doing well. Acknowledging them for that action will encourage them to want to keep trying and doing more of the new habit.

This is a good lesson for managers and team leaders who are trying to get teams or individuals to increase their work performance. The typical manager is often quick to point out what's not going well and rarely looks at what is going well. Sometimes, management uses the sandwich technique where they give one piece of encouragement followed by telling them what they're doing wrong followed by another piece of positive acknowledgement. You may hear it go like this:

"Hi John, thanks for coming in today, I've noticed that you seem to be making extra calls, well done. However, they don't seem to be turning into leads at present, which, if it continues, is going to be a problem for you. I've noticed that you don't seem to be able to close any deals, I guess that's where you need to do some work. Anyway, keep doing your best, I know you're trying hard."

The manager sees this as praise. However, all John heard was that he's not closing any deals and this is going to be a problem! If John is trying to build a new habit of making more calls and closing more deals, telling him he's not doing very well won't encourage him to continue on with the new habit. John may have increased his call rate by fifty per cent, however, the manager only focused on what he hasn't achieved. In addition, it is likely that John is already being hard on himself. He could already be having a conversation with himself about what he's not doing well. The manager's sandwich style of feedback might cause John to think that what he said may be true and that he'll never be able to change. This can flow into other areas of his work performance, compounding an already difficult change for John.

This is not to say that only praise is the option. Particularly if failure to change can result in breaking the law or perhaps be physically harmful. There is a time and place where discipline is necessary. My point is, however, that we tend to be far more critical of performance than to choose to offer praise. We tend to look out for what is not going well, instead of looking out for what is going well.

It is understood that to improve and keep performance high, we should offer praise to criticism at a ratio of five to one. For every one criticism, we should praise five times. Keep in mind it is likely that the individual has already been critical of themselves, so you will be adding to this self-criticism each time.

Without self-acknowledgement and without recognition from others, it is very difficult to create new habits.

Creating a nurturing environment

Not only do we need a lot of encouragement from ourselves and others, we also need to create a physical space around us to avoid falling back on our past habits. When attempting to create new habits, we must consider the environment around us as well as other people. This may include the people we currently associate with, it could be the way we organise our desks or even the way we dress. It is difficult to create the new habit of exercise three times per week if we don't have the correct clothing. Likewise, it is going to be hard to increase your call numbers if you are surrounded by mess and clutter.

The people you have around you can also have a big impact on your ability to create new positive habits. When you begin to create these habits, you may need to change what you do or perhaps what you say. It's important that if the new habits you're looking to create may have an effect on others that are close to you, you should let them know what it is you're trying to change. This will allow them the opportunity to encourage and assist you when necessary and to understand that what you're trying to do can be difficult.

The more supporters you have, the easier it will be to create the new habits. Let's say you're trying meet more people through networking events. This may require you to go out after hours or perhaps on your days off. Having your family and friends understand this will help them to adjust to changes they may have to make to help you achieve this. This is particularly valid if the results of the new positive habits will ultimately have a positive outcome for them as well.

The opposite to this is that some people might not want you to change. This can be because they feel you're perfect the way you are or that your changing may force change upon them. In a work situation where you are trying to increase productivity, there may be individuals who will want you to fail so that their performance doesn't come under the spotlight. They may try to hold you back in subtle ways like trying to distract you. They may be more obvious and tell you that what you're trying to do is stupid or a waste of time.

Becoming aware of who around you is supporting the new positive habit and who is not is vitally important. Once you have established this, you can decide in what circles you travel and who is helpful and who is a hindrance. Obviously, in a work environment or family situation, you can't just remove yourself from these people; however, becoming mindful of who they are can help you decide who to spend more or less time hanging around with.

These are just a few examples of things that can increase the challenge of creating new habits. In the next chapter,

I will talk about goals and what actions you can take that will support any new habits you need.

My Top 5 Lessons

1. **Recognise and acknowledge the habits you want to change and write them down**
2. **Be one hundred per cent committed to change**
3. **Craft actions to complete to create the new habit and write them down**
4. **Support and acknowledge the new positive habits**
5. **Surround yourself with people who will cheer you on with your new habits**

The training trap

I'm one of the biggest advocates of training. From as far back as I can remember, I have attended countless training courses, seminars and workshops. When I started in real estate, main events were held such as the Australian real estate conference and several well-known real estate trainers offered a variety of courses. Subjects ranging from the basic principles of selling, through to learning all the scripts and dialogues that you will ever encounter in real estate were covered. I've attended most that was on offer. You can add to this list the training we all need for compliance to maintain registrations and licences that are necessary to keep updated with the latest legislation and changes to real estate law.

I remember attending my first real estate conference, which showcased some great speakers from within the industry and others outside. One that I remember clearly had Tom O'Toole speaking about his success as the owner of the Beechworth Bakery. A straight talker, Tom shared some fantastic insights, many of which could be applied to real estate. He spoke a great deal about the importance of training and retraining his staff and it being one of the critical success points of his business. One quote that stood out, however, was that one day he was asked: "Tom, what if you do all this training with your staff and they leave? His response? "What if I don't train them and they stay!" I heard this quip about ten years ago and I still remember it to this day.

It is important that we continually train to learn and up-skill. The way in which we conduct ourselves in real estate has changed dramatically during the past 20 years. A great example of this is the advent of the internet and all the property information that's now available online. No longer are agents the holder of all the information; the general public can now obtain all the same data agents can and this has changed the way we conduct our business. Just learning the scripts and dialogues is no longer enough.

As new agents enter the market, they need to learn certain important things that don't change, such as the ability to connect with new clients that one day may sell, the skills required to nurture these relationships until they are ready to sell and the skills needed to successfully negotiate offers into sales. Learning how to complete sales agreements and contracts is also important and the list goes on and on. The need for constant training is critical within this rapidly evolving industry, particularly in the area of social media where Facebook, Twitter, LinkedIn and the like are gaining traction among agents and clients alike.

The great part about training is that it takes you out of your environment and puts you into a place with similar like-minded people who are willing to learn. It's an inspiring, often fun and exciting place. It is also an opportunity to get out of the office.

Where training tends to fall down, however, is in the implementation of the skills learnt. The ability to turn the new learning into new sustainable habits is critical. Unless this training becomes a new habit, the old habits will eventually come back and nothing will change. Or at best, only short-term change will occur. This then put us into a training cycle where we consistently learn the same things and implement very little or nothing at all.

For training to be truly useful, the skills to *implement*

the new learning must be learnt. After all, without implementation, training becomes just moments of inspiration and motivation. The problem with both of these is that eventually the energy runs out and nothing changes.

If the new training isn't nurtured and practiced, the current thinking will prevail, as will the current habits. The current training models barely touch on the actions required to implement the changes. It is left up to the individual or group to simply change course and begin to do something new, hope that nothing gets in the way and that the old habits don't take over. Chances are that, over time, without the continual support of the new learning, little if nothing at all will be followed through.

Ultimately, because the support for the new habits has not occurred, the old habits remain and there is no progress. The temptation is to continue to do more training and hope that the result will be different. Of course, the result is more of the same.

Continual training is important, but more important is the *implementation* of what is learnt.

My Top 5 Lessons
1. **Never stop training**
2. **Be open minded to new learning**
3. **Training creates energy – learn to harness that energy**
4. **Mix up real estate training with other complementary training**
5. **The power of training is in the implementation: Training + Action = Success**

3

BIG BOLD JUICY GOALS

"Vision without action is a daydream.
Action without vision is a nightmare."
– Japanese proverb

The importance of goals

Most seminars that focus around change, up-skilling, creating new etc will at some point talk about goals. Every weight loss program, book or workshop will ask you to identify your goals. What would *you* like to achieve? Doing so takes you into the future and gets you to look at what it is that you want when you're done. The simple ones to identify are goals like: "I want to pay off my mortgage by the time I'm 40" or "I want to fit into my wedding dress for that special day". The great thing about having goals is it keeps you focused on what it is you want, especially when things get tough.

The US Navy Seals are encouraged to set goals. Through much research and study into Neuroscience, the Navy Seals discovered that having goals helps them to achieve their objectives at a much higher rate. Setting goals keeps them looking at the long-term objective versus the short-term pain. Using goal setting helped decrease the massive dropout rate during training, increasing the number of Seals passing their extreme physical and mental tests.

We can learn from this study by understanding that if we look towards a future that is well-defined, the hurdles that we will inevitably encounter are easier to overcome. Success comes when you are looking at the bigger picture.

Perhaps your goal is to run your first marathon. You decide that this will become the focus of your training over the course of the next weeks, months or perhaps years. It may be something you have wanted to do for a long time and have never really committed to doing.

This is where most people start and finish when setting their goals. It's great you now have something to aim for but there is a very high chance that you won't get there. Why? There are several factors.

Top three mistakes when setting goals

Mistake 1 – Lack of planning

So I'm going to run a marathon. I start running five times per week for 30 minutes, then increase that to an hour at a time, and then start running 10km, then 20km, then 40km. Sorted. Maybe, maybe not.

Using marathon training as an example, let's follow Adam on his quest to run a marathon.

Adam lets his family know that he is going to start training and he sets his alarm for a 6am start Monday morning. Six am comes and the alarm goes off! He reaches over and hits the off button, ready to go. Just before he jumps out of bed, his wife comes closer for a snuggle and encourages him to stay, it's cold out there. As tempting as it is, Adam is committed to his goal and jumps up and begins to get ready. After a few minutes, he has pulled on his clothes and runners and in the morning sunrise heads off doing a slow jog, he's under way.

A few hundred metres down the road, Adam is starting to feel his muscles work for the first time in years; it's a challenge but he feels pretty good. He hits the 1km mark and, apart from a little discomfort in his knees and feet, he's happy with his progress. The 2km mark comes and goes and he's starting to draw in some heavy breaths, he doesn't remember it being this hard when he played football. At the 3km mark, his feet are getting really sore but he's tough and pushes through, he's determined to do his first 5km. At 4km, he's slowed down to a shuffle, his feet are now killing him and he feels like his heart is about to pound through his chest, but home is now in sight. With only 1km to go, Adam is now as red as a tomato, sucking in every last piece of oxygen and cursing his feet to move, but he's nearly there. At last, he shuffles the final few steps up the driveway and collapses on the front lawn.

While he sprawls there, contemplating how good it is to be home, he slowly returns to normal and makes his way inside. His wife greets him with enthusiasm and is quick to encourage his tremendous efforts. Being such a great wife, as a reward she has also prepared him his favourite breakfast of bacon and eggs, which he quickly devours as he finally recovers.

Although it was a tough slog, he still feels committed to his goal and he's all ready to go again the next morning.

When the alarm goes off the next day at 6am, Adam rolls over ready to go. Just as he puts his feet down, he realises that his legs are so sore he can barely stand and lets out a groan. Not only are his legs sore, he has developed huge blisters on his heels, which also cause him pain. Hearing all the moaning, his wife rolls over and encourages him to have the day off for a rest. Adam's determination to stick with his fitness training is strong, however his body doesn't seem to want to cooperate. He agrees with his wife and crawls back into bed, muttering that a few days off shouldn't do any harm.

As you can see in this example, Adam had great intentions, but he failed to spend the time planning how he was going to get from where he was to where he wanted to be. This is often where most people fail when it comes to setting goals. This is why New Year's resolutions don't work. Without a plan, you are set to fail from the beginning.

Goals often end up involving others such as work colleagues, friends or partners. When setting goals, it's important to recognise that these are *your goals* and not other people's. Without careful planning, you may not realise that other people's involvement may be critical to your success in achieving your outcomes. An example of this, perhaps you're wanting to change careers. In doing so, you come to realise that you will need to do a lot of study after hours. This may conflict with your partner's schedule, or the kid's activities and could easily derail your goal.

Planning is one of the most critical steps in setting goals and there should be plenty of time spent in this area.

Mistake 2 – Lack of clarity

A goal must be well-defined and easily measured. It is easy to sit around and dream about what it is you would like. You may even have a picture in your mind of what it looks like, but if you can't define exactly what it is you want and by when, it will most likely stay a dream. A goal must be exciting and inspiring. The journey towards your goal can often be challenging and difficult, depending on what it is. So the more excited you are about achieving your goals, the easier it is to work through the tough stages. After all, the idea of setting a goal is to achieve something you have wanted but has been out of reach to date. If it wasn't going to be a challenge, you would have achieved it already.

A goal must be able to be measured. Otherwise, how will you know if you are there or how close you have gotten? There are two main ways to measure goals, one more tangible than the other. One is simple, like a number: I have paid $20,000 off my mortgage; I now weigh 70kg; I have completed my first triathlon. These are easily measured. The more challenging measures are around feelings. Wanting to be happy, or successful or fulfilled. These still need to be measured and are equally valid as goals.

Mistake 3 – Lack of will

Creating change is hard, at times very hard. After all, if it was easy there would be no need for a book like this. You must be one hundred per cent committed to the change you want; it has to be constantly on your radar. Without the will to change, you are likely to fail. As humans, we are programmed to retreat to safety whenever something gets difficult. It was built into us through evolution to help ensure our survival as a race. The urge to stop and stay safe will always be a temptation. As will making excuses as to why you didn't achieve what you wanted to change.

Without incredible resolve and a belief that what you want is better than what you already have, in most cases, you won't succeed. Given that we spend the majority of our lives creating all that we are, to turn around and start to redo new things takes a massive amount of willpower. It's not as simple as saying it over and over and it will be so. There needs to be an overwhelming desire to want to change. From time to time, we are faced with the need to change, regardless of what we may want. This may be true with your health. If the doctor were to advise you that unless you lost weight you would be dead within a year, you would have a much greater chance to lose the weight. You would find the will to do what is required to survive.

The desire to change can't be overstated in any way. Without this as the core component in the process of change, you will be drawn back to a place of comfort and safety and ultimately remain where you are.

How goals improve productivity and performance

As humans, we need a purpose in life. For some of us, making millions is the dream, for others perhaps happiness is what they strive for and, for some, having their football team win is their purpose. It doesn't matter what it is, there has to be a purpose. Without purpose, there is little to look forward to and life becomes pretty miserable. When it comes to work, there are a lucky few that love their job, really love their job. What they do at work is their purpose and it is a large part of who they are and why they exist. For many others, however, work is a means to an end, a way to get what we want. You may really enjoy what you do but there is a bigger picture, dream or purpose most are looking for.

Some of the happiest people in the world live in third world countries, have very few possessions and live in comparatively poor conditions. Studies have shown that their happiness is derived from their higher purpose, which in most cases is their family and communities. It's based on their ability to contribute to a greater common good.

The problem for most of us is that we don't actually know what that purpose is or what it is that is more important than work. Sure, most would acknowledge that family and friends are the most important thing and takes precedence over work. However, most of us spend a larger part of our awake time working and not where we see our purpose as being. One of the greatest benefits in setting and working towards a goal or goals is to shift the focus from the day-to-day tasks of work to a higher purpose: the reason why we actually go to work. The majority of people I meet are not inspired by money – in fact, it ranks quite low on their priorities. It is usually what money can do for them that is the attraction: independence, holidays with family, nicer home etc, is what they work towards.

Not having a clear picture of what it is you want can make great days merely good – and bad days really bad. You start to question what it is you're doing and why you're doing it. Situations can become overwhelming and the urge to give up can grow, resulting in poor performance and sometimes quitting all together. You may find yourself questioning your ability to do the job even though you may have years of experience. You may even find yourself moving from job to job, searching for what it is that will give you purpose when all along it lies within yourself.

Establishing goals will move your thinking to a higher level. It will shift your focus from the day-to-day tasks and keep you looking at the big picture. When there is a goal or purpose that is bigger than the individual tasks, you will find yourself in a completely different state of mind. Suddenly, the wins become even more exciting because they are the steps to achieving the greater goal. And with each success, you gain momentum and reinforce new positive habits that keep moving you towards your goals.

Let's consider a football team at the beginning of the season. If their focus was solely on the individual game and they experienced a loss, this would start to create negative thinking that would affect their results in subsequent games. Moving the focus to the end game or the grand final keeps the focus at a higher level. It gives the players something to work towards, regardless of the results of the individual games.

The same can be said for real estate. If we don't have a greater purpose, the habits that support rejection, failure and loss will override our mental state, after all, these lows are part of the real estate agent's career and any sales related career. Having a goal to work towards will keep the focus high for when there are setbacks and rejection, which will then allow the agent to recover faster with much less potential to accept failure or rejection. The result of this, of course, is higher productivity and performance.

Knowing why they are working long hours, making tough calls and experiencing rejection is critical to the high performing agent. They will experience these setbacks equal to any others, but the difference is they will keep their attention on the end game. In doing so, any setback washes off easier, ready to move to the next deal or opportunity. They can maintain the right level of mental fitness needed to stay consistent around the core habits required for high performance. High performing real estate agents understand that having goals removes the pressure to perform. Having goals gives certainty to the high performer in what is often a high stress environment. They have a very clear path to follow and know what needs to be done. There is no time wasted floundering around deciding what should be done next. They can plan weeks and months in advance, which stops the boom and bust cycle experienced by the average agent.

Knowing what it is you want can help you understand what's working well for you in supporting the existing habits. It helps you see what's missing from your current habits or skills that will be needed to reach the goals. It also helps highlight what's not going well so that certain habits can be broken or adjusted. This understanding will keep you moving forward. Determining goals from the beginning saves a lot of wasted time down the track. Understanding what you want, where you are coming from and how you are going to get there is a key element to maintaining high productivity and performance.

Having others around you understand what is it that you're working towards will help support the goals as well. Real estate can involve many long hours and can affect other people such as family and other key relationships. Having them know what your purpose is will allow them to support what it is you want. Without this involvement, they could perceive the long hours and high stress as not being worthwhile. They can see that all the effort does have a purpose and benefit to them as well, particularly when they are a part of the purpose. Similarly, having set goals, you will be able to recognise those who are holding you back, the people that are getting in the way. They may not have seemed obvious prior to the goal and most will be well-meaning. They can be obvious like those who tell you "it can't be done" or, less so, those who can be distracting when you are working to complete tasks.

When working in a group or team environment, people can consciously and unconsciously try to hold you back. When you begin to rise above the pack, the light begins to shine upon them and their average performance. Their instinct will be to stop you from changing and try and keep you where you are. This may happen in subtle ways such as minor interruptions, or general banter that takes your attention away from your greater purpose. It can be very obvious when others may criticise what you are doing and try and encourage you to see things their way. These are all ways to try and have you conform and stop you from changing.

When you have a clear understanding of what it is you want, what goals you are focused on, others will have little impact on your determination to achieve what you want. You will develop habits that won't allow for the distractions and only allow for positive relationships.

What are goals?

Goals are simply something that we want to achieve. Goals draw your attention to something specific that you may have thought about for a long time or perhaps has just been a distant dream. As a coach, I work with individuals and teams to create great goals that they can work on over the course of our coaching engagement. There are several parts to setting meaningful goals:

1. They should be inspiring and exciting and make you feel motivated thinking about them.

2. A goal should be written. Writing your goals down will make you far more likely to achieve them and it will keep them present at all times.

3. A goal needs to be specific and not vague. You need to be very clear about what it is you want to achieve.

   For example:
   - Unclear goal – I want to make more sales.

   - Clear goal – I want to achieve ten more sales.

4. A goal must have a measure; after all, you need to know how you are progressing and when you've reached your goal. There are several ways to measure a goal, depending on what the goal is. However, the most common measure is with a number or a clearly defined end point or by a feeling.

For example:
- I want to reduce my debt by thirty per cent (number)

- I want to feel happiness like I did at my twenty-first birthday bash (feeling)

    Both goals have a measure but in different ways.

5. A goal must have a completion date. When will the goal be complete by? If you want to establish a goal that could take months or even years, you may want to break this down into smaller goals.

    For example:
- I want to buy a house in five years' time

    An alternative goal might be:

- I'll have a $20,000 deposit saved in six months

6. A goal should be a challenge but also realistic. If there is little or no challenge, you are likely to get bored and not worry about it. If the goal is highly unlikely or impossible, you won't be able to convince yourself it is worthwhile.

7. A goal must have a series of strategies and actions that move you towards the outcome.

8. Goals should be celebrated to encourage and acknowledge all the new learning for the future.

9. Goals can be established in many areas of your life.

It is worthwhile setting goals in different areas of your life at the same time to create balance. Goals can be challenging and, by having goals in different areas, you are more likely to have at least one goal going well, no matter what is going on in other areas.

Some examples of areas to set goals include:

- Work
- Health
- Financial
- Business
- Creative
- Career
- Relationships

Goals are not KPIs

It's very common for many sales oriented people to have a set of goals they are working towards. The essence of sales is to sell products or services and usually towards a target or a predefined outcome. These outcomes are usually calculated at the beginning of the sales cycle with benchmarks set along the way. In real estate and many other industries, these are usually referred to as Key Performance Indicators or KPIs and are a series of numbers or targets that the individual or team is working towards.

These numbers are then used to track the continual performance of the individual or team to gauge their success or failure against the particular outcome.

For example:
- Minimum number of appraisals = 100 per year
- Minimum number of listings = 50 per year
- Minimum number of sales = 30 per year
- Total dollar value of commission $200,000

Note that dozens of KPIs can be tracked, these are just a few examples.

Tracking these numbers is critical to the sales person and their organisation, as this will help them understand if they are on or off track and need to make adjustments to their numbers.

Most high performing agents and their offices will watch these numbers closely throughout the year. High performing agents often benchmark themselves against what they achieved in previous years and against other individuals or offices in the same field.

Understanding the numbers and what effect they have on the outcome can't be underestimated. Knowing the numbers helps with planning for time off, planning for more training, budgeting for marketing and so on. The problem is that they are often used as or referred to as 'goals' to be achieved. They are definitely something to achieve but they do not meet the definition of a goal.

A goal must be inspiring and motivating for the individual or team. In the case of a team, the goal must be agreed upon by the whole team. Simply setting and tracking KPIs as the goals is unlikely to motivate and inspire the individual or team. Achieving the KPIs may be a step in the possible achievement of the goal – but they are not the goal.

We have to move a few steps beyond this point and ask what would be possible if we achieved these KPIs? This is the beginning of establishing goals.

For example:
- If you were to hit your KPIs, what effect would it have on your financial situation?
- If you were to hit your KPIs, what effect would it have on your ability to travel?
- If you were to hit your KPI's, what effect would it have on your relationships?

The KPIs themselves are not the goals. They are just one step or a strategy towards what may inspire and excite you. It's important not to confuse the two.

The 4 easy steps to creating great goals

Often when people set about creating a goal or goals, they will have something in mind to achieve. It could be something that has been hanging around for a long time, like travel, or a great relationship or perhaps financial independence.

For example:

You may have been thinking about going overseas for some years and it's been years since you've had a great break, so you have decided to arrange a holiday. This might be where you decide to set a goal.

or

You have just had a second child so your house is getting too small. You may decide to set a goal about moving to a larger home.

These are great goals and well worth going for. As discussed, however, there are many things that make up a goal and, without taking the appropriate steps, the chances of succeeding are very low or perhaps you will fall well short. Unfortunately, this is very common and often why people fail to continue to set goals. Perhaps they have tried to set a goal once or twice and after their attempts fail, give up on setting goals again. Or they convince themselves that goal setting just doesn't work.

The steps outlined below are what I follow when establishing a new goal for an individual or team. The only difference between the two is that the team has a common goal that they all share.

This example also applies to an individual or team that doesn't necessarily have a goal in mind. I'll show you how to start from scratch, because it's good to understand how to establish a goal from scratch as you may want to apply this goal-setting technique to other areas in your life, not just your career. In fact, as discussed already, it is highly recommended that you do take the time to think about and set a variety of goals. Working as a coach, I often find that once a coachee sets their goals, as they begin to work through the tasks required to complete these goals, new and more exciting goals can crop up – and these are the goals that become the most life-changing and inspiring. The point is that the action of setting goals can really open up your mind and help you determine your heart's true desires and your life purpose. After all, setting goals is all about figuring out what is you want and what it is you no longer want in your life.

Step 1 – List all the areas in your life

Start by making a list of all the areas in your life in dot points. Spend plenty of time getting this done and make sure there's nothing left out. These aren't just the areas that you may want to work on but your whole life. Later, we will start deleting what you're satisfied with.

Look at areas like work, family, relationships, travel, religion, career, hobbies, sport, kids, health, spirituality, etc. Start to list them like the example below.

I like to go to the gym	I ride a road bike	I live in a nice neighbourhood
I enjoy BBQs with friends	I am a Real Estate agent	I want to travel to Europe
I have two children	I'd like to publish a children's book	I enjoy photography
I like good food	I want to retire when I am 55	I'd like to earn more money
I enjoy time on my own	I have great friends	I want to learn Yoga
I would like to lose 10kg	I'd like to get a business degree	My partner works too much

Step 2 – Group similar areas together

Using the same list, you can start to group areas that go together. This will start to refine the different areas of your life.

Health:	**Personal:**
I like to go to the gym	I enjoy time on my own
I want to learn Yoga	I've got two children
I'd like to lose 10kg	I ride a road bike
	I enjoy BBQ's with friends
	I've got great friends
	My partner works too much
Work/Career:	**Leisure/Pleasure:**
I'd like to get a business degree	I would like to publish a children's book
I'd like to earn more money	I enjoy photography
I am a Real Estate agent	
I want to retire when I am 55	

Step 3 – Choose areas to work on

Start by highlighting the area or areas you would like to work on most. This is the beginning of where you may want to set a goal.

Health:	**Personal:**
I like to go to the gym	I enjoy time on my own
I want to learn Yoga	I've got two children
I'd like to lose 10kg	I ride a road bike
	I enjoy BBQ's with friends
	I've got great friends
	My partner works too much
Work/Career:	**Leisure/Pleasure:**
I'd like to get a business degree	I would like to publish a children's book
I'd like to earn more money	I enjoy photography
I am a Real Estate agent	
I want to retire when I am 55	

Step 4 – Polishing the goal

Now you have done all the hard work establishing the areas you would like to work on, it's time to turn these into inspiring and exciting goals. Thinking about how the future will look once you have achieved these goals will help you redefine how the goal might sound.

For example:

Good goal – I'd like to lose 10kg
Great goal – I will fit into my dinner suit for the June Ball

Good goal – I'd like to earn more money
Great goal – My house deposit is ready There is $20,000 in the bank.

Good goal – I'd like to publish a children's book
Great goal – I've completed three book launches by December

Each of the goals are looked at from the future and have clear measures against them. Although you might feel a little unsure, there should be some excitement about these goals. An excitement in knowing that, should you achieve these things, you'll feel a great sense of accomplishment. You should also feel that achieving the goals will be a stretch; after all, if they weren't, it is likely you would have achieved them already. It's not important to concern yourself with *how* it is going to happen, just that it *will*, and that the results are going to be fantastic.

Don't rush these steps, as they will become the foundation for what you are working towards over the coming weeks and months. Once you feel great about your new goals, it is time to start planning. This will be the road map that will take you from where you are now to where you want to be in the future. Like spending the time crafting great goals, spending the time to plan the steps to the goals is equally important.

Breaking it down into big chunks

Once you have crafted a great inspiring goal that you are one hundred per cent committed to, then it is time to break it down into strategies or big steps and then actions. The idea of breaking the goal down is to get a clearer look at how you are going to achieve it and to clarify the areas you need to work on to achieve your goals. By breaking down the goal, you will see the goal starting to come to life. Be excited as it begins to become very real. There are several areas you need to develop strategies in to ensure you have all the steps needed to be successful.

Your current reality

Before you can head off to achieve your inspiring goal, you need to understand where you are and what is your current reality. This is what and who you are right now. We very rarely stop and think about what is going on around us. This step will make you look at your existing habits and ascertain if they will assist you in moving towards your goal or hold you back. Knowing where you are develops the foundation of where you are coming from and will allow you to start to think of what you already have. Going through this process will also help you flesh out what you may need to do more of. What are the things that you are doing well that will support you moving towards your goal? Your current reality will also have you look at what is missing or doesn't currently exist. This will help highlight areas that you may need to improve upon or start doing to achieve your goal.

Understanding your current reality will form the foundation from which you can start to create the changes you need to achieve you goals.

Planning

The planning stage of goal setting is vitally important to ensure the eventual outcomes of your goals. It is important to spend all the time necessary planning to craft the stages you will need to get closer to your goal. When in the planning stage, look from the future rather than the present. Coming from the future will help you design the steps you would take to achieve that goal.

Starting with the goal, begin to imagine what it looks like to have finally achieved what it is you want. Picture yourself already being that person, having now completed the goal successfully. Spend some time seeing yourself in that place. Think about how you feel and what you are doing. Who is around you and what do you look like? This is the place to get in touch with your future. The easier you can see what it is you have become, the easier it will be to begin to plan the steps needed to achieve your goals.

Once you can see yourself having completed the goal, start to write down the big steps or strategies you took to achieve it. Try not to get into too much detail at this stage. You are looking for chunks that will be later broken down into smaller actions. As you are writing down the steps, think of these as a series of actions. If what you write down can be completed in one or two steps, it is likely to be an action rather than a strategy.

For example:

Goal: Drinking a coffee in Italy

Strategy: Create a budget (current reality)

Action: Get the past three months' bank statements

Action: Block out time to plan the budget

Action: Arrange to meet my travel partner to discuss costs

Action: Check current savings

Action: Create a list of current expenses

Using this as an example, you can see that the strategy of 'Create a budget' will involve many different steps each only requiring one action. There can be a temptation to quickly get into the action steps but it's important to stay out of the detail until the big steps are mostly in place. Sometimes, upon having completed the strategies and getting into action, you might discover another area is missing. You can add new strategies at any time if you feel it will be part of your journey to the goal.

Setting strategies can sometimes be difficult as we tend to have trouble seeing the big picture. Remember that you are creating new thinking so it can be difficult. If you find yourself diving into the detail, go back to the future and work backwards. Often in coaching, we ask our clients to imagine they have bumped into someone they haven't seen for a while and that person asks them how they achieved their goal. Imagine what you would say. What were the big milestones that got you from the past to the future? You are looking for at least six to eight big steps to form your strategies. Once you have these written down and you feel like there are no gaps, it is time to move into action.

Crafting simple actions

So now that you have developed an exciting and inspiring goal and outlined the big steps for how to get there, it is time to get into action. Actions – unlike strategies – are the small steps that will lead you to the completion of the strategies. Actions should be able to be completed in a short period, hours or days versus weeks. If you find that the actions require more than one step, break them down even further. Actions must also have a completion date; when will the action be done by? This creates commitment around the action to get things done. Also, through the completion of the actions, you may unearth other actions that need to be completed to move towards the strategy.

For example:

Goal: Run the Sydney Marathon

Strategy: Gather all the training equipment

Action with multiple steps: Buy running shoes

Single action: Research suitable shoes online – Thurs night between eight and nine o'clock

Single action: Talk to another runner about shoe types – Saturday at running club

Single action: Block out time to go to shoe store in lunch break – Block out Monday lunch for 45 min.

By breaking down the actions to one simple step at a time, each action becomes easily achievable.

As you complete the actions, ask yourself "what's next?" or "what else?" You should constantly review your actions to make sure you haven't left anything out. As you work through completing your actions, you will have a great sense of achievement. Completing the actions creates new habits of getting things done. The more actions you complete, the easier it will become to get things done as those positive habits are created.

The other great outcome about getting into action is that you will begin to notice what's NOT getting done. If there are actions you are creating to move yourself towards your goal and you are constantly avoiding doing those things, or doing them less than one hundred per cent, you need to reflect on those actions. Is there something you first thought you wanted but now doesn't seem that important? Ask yourself "Am I avoiding the action because I'm afraid of the outcome?" "Am I finding it difficult to complete my actions because I'm trying to do something completely new and unfamiliar?" All these questions are valid and may arise at any stage of the process.

Any or all of these things can be true. Listening to yourself through this process is important as part of the journey to achieving your goals. By discovering that something you thought you wanted is no longer important for now, or at all, you will be free to place your energy in other areas. Similarly, finding some actions to be difficult or a stretch is also a sign that you're well underway to creating the change you've wanted and achieving your goals.

Example goal showing strategies and actions:

Goal: "I am number one in the office"
Strategy (current reality): I know my numbers (KPIs)

Actions:
- Get a list of the past 12 months' sales – Monday
- Print a list of past clients – Wednesday afternoon
- Break down conversion rates – Saturday
- Print a list of competitors' market share – Thursday morning 8–10am

Strategy: I trained
Actions:
- Research different coaches on the internet – Wednesday night after 8pm
- Block out dates for next local sales conference – Lunch time Tuesday
- Go to book store to look for training books – Lunch time Tuesday
- Ask my manager for office training resources – Sales meeting Wednesday morning

Strategy: I had a network of high performers around me
Actions:
- Research social media for people in similar roles and connect with a minimum of five – Wednesday
- Look up local business meeting dates – Tuesday after work
- Put the next six months of local business dates into my calendar – Friday
- Look for books written about high achievers – Tuesday at 5pm

Strategy: I was financially stable
Actions:
- Write a list of all my costs and expenses – Sunday
- Draft a budget – Sunday
- Make a list of costs I can cut – Thursday night, after 8pm
- Calculate the additional sales needed to accumulate three months of savings in bank – Monday 4pm

Strategy: I did the hard work
Actions:
- Make a list of daily tasks I do – Wednesday 3–5pm
- Prioritise work order of money-making tasks – Tuesday afternoon
- Block out diary with non-negotiable activities – Monday
- Plan regular down time once per month in diary – Monday

Strategy: Family and friends were onboard
Actions:
- Have a meeting with my partner regarding my goals – Tuesday night
- Share my goals with my best friends – Next weekend
- Write a list of activities my partner can help me with – Saturday
- Put up pictures of family and friends in my office as reminders – Friday

Strategy (celebration): I'm on my way to Europe for three weeks
Actions
- Get travel brochures from travel agent – Lunch Wednesday
- Look at three potential dates to travel – Tuesday 7pm
- Compile a list of countries I'd like to visit – Sunday
- Check passports are current – Sunday

As you can see in this example, the actions require just one step and have a completion date against them. You may find yourself doing more actions in some areas than others. There is no 'right' number of actions – just enough to complete the strategy. As you complete your actions, ask yourself "what's next?" or" "what else?" and continue to craft actions. As you work through this process, you may find it more and more difficult to come up with new actions. If you find yourself stuck, you may want to leave that area and come back to it later. You may find that by completing other actions, you may get ideas about actions needed in other areas.

It's a great idea to keep your goals handy as you may come up with some great actions when you are least expecting it. Write them down and add them to your goals as soon as practical.

Celebrate

After all the planning and hard work and now having achieved your goals, it's time to celebrate. The celebration is an important part of your journey in achieving your goals. Not only does it give you something to look forward to, by taking the time to acknowledge your successes, you help reinforce the new positive habits you have created. The way you celebrate is entirely up to you, but it is important to do it your way; after all, you've achieved the goals. Your celebration may include others at a dinner, party or perhaps an outing or it can be private, enjoying something special just for yourself. No matter how you celebrate, the thing that matters the most is that it is what you want and something you will look forward to.

4

INCREDIBLE PRODUCTIVITY

> *"The difference between a successful person and others, is not a lack of strength, not a lack of knowledge. But rather a lack of will."*
> – Vince Lombardi

Many great resources – written and spoken – are available when it comes to productivity, effectiveness, efficiency and high performance. Many business books are written about this topic and play a vital role in training groups and individuals on how to use their time in the most productive way in a practical sense. Others combine both the physical changes you can make to increase productivity with mental preparation. These books talk about mindfulness and becoming aware of what's going on in our thinking under different circumstances. They also cover influences on how we react in different situations, how our mood affects our performance and even understanding how different personalities react to different situations. All of these factors play a vital role in becoming a high performing agent, but many only spend time in one or two places from time to time.

There are three main areas that require constant attention and growth to become a high performing highly productive agent:

- Healthy lifestyle
- Efficient and organised physical space and systems
- Mental control and mindfulness

There is no doubt that when it comes to real estate, high performers have a great balance of both physical and mental preparedness. Physical preparedness relates to both ourselves and our heath as well as our physical space, or the environment we live and work in.

Your physical health

I'm not an expert in health and fitness and this is not about telling you what to eat and how to exercise. I did however spend more than ten years as a fitness instructor and personal trainer and I continue to live a healthy, active life. It is generally accepted that the healthier we are, the better we cope with stress and decision-making.

Eating well

This is the core of where all our energy comes from and, without a healthy balanced diet, it is not possible to function consistently at a high level day in day out. We need to prepare for the challenges we come across throughout the day and the mental stresses we must deal with. As we think at a high level, we draw physical energy out of the body and this needs to be replaced on a regular basis. High level thinking such as problem solving lowers blood sugar levels and without re-fuelling as we go through the day, your energy level will drop, affecting your performance.

Like other activities of a high performing agent, they spend time planning their meals so they don't skip or miss out on meals throughout the day. One of the biggest problems I see is agents not eating healthy food or skipping meals altogether. This will have a dramatic impact on your day. Taking the time to plan and prepare your meals will help avoid delaying eating or worse still not eating at all. Having food with you as snacks in the car or on your desk is a great way to keep energy up throughout the day. Spending time the night before getting meals together will help avoid the need to buy fast food.

Regular exercise

Like most things discussed in this book, exercise is a habit. The most important thing when it comes to exercise is to do *something*. Over the years, I've played sport, gone to the gym, done triathlons. I have tried just about most things. What I have learnt, is that you need to do something that you enjoy and do it regularly. The problem for most people who don't exercise regularly is not what they do but the lack of consistency in what they do. Finding what works for you is the key. This may seem simple, however it comes back to listening to yourself and doing what feels right. If you don't believe in what you're doing, it can't become a habit and you won't continue with it.

If you are new to exercise, consult a professional like a personal trainer or join a group exercise program so you can receive proper instruction. Maybe join a sporting club or meet a friend for a regular walk if it works for you. You don't have to be obsessed about it and you don't have to become a marathon runner. Just remember to do some exercise and stick at it.

Exercise is not only important for our physical heath but also our mental health. It's a great way to refocus our minds away from work and other stresses and give ourselves a mental rest. Take some time to plan your regular exercise program and daily meals. Being in great physical shape will add significant value to your real estate career and, without it, it is not possible to become a high performer. Without your physical health, you have nothing. No work, no friends no family. A great career, money or lifestyle cannot take the place of good health, because without it you have nothing.

Your physical environment

Without great systems and procedures, you will be forever struggling to keep pace with the workload of a high performer. As your business grows, the ability to have systems take care of repetitive tasks becomes critically important. Creating a physical space with automated systems will support a fast-growing individual real estate business. This will allow you to stay focused on the dollar producing activities necessary to be a high performer. Spending time getting all the physical areas of your business in order will not only enable you to produce much larger volumes with less effort, you will also be under less pressure, which will support your mental state.

Personal preparation

Dress

If you want to be a high performer, you need to dress like one. Investing in clothes that will represent you and your market place is important to show your clients that you look equipped for the job. This doesn't mean you need to spend a fortune on expensive suits or shoes, but that your clothes fit well and are clean. It means your shoes aren't all worn, scuffed and falling apart. You are selling most people's most valuable asset and you should dress accordingly. If you dress like you are a high performer, you will begin to feel like one. Dressing smartly will support your mental state by looking like the high performer you want to be. You will support the thinking that you are well on your way.

Car

Like your clothes, your car needs to be well-presented and clean, inside and out. Cleaning your car of dirt and clutter will not only have you looking like a high performer but will also have a relaxing effect on your mind. Each time you jump into a car full of clutter, you will, either on a conscious or subconscious level, have a sense of frustration that you need to tidy up. A small thing but a mental distraction you can do without.

Your work space

High performers understand that to get things done, they need an orderly and systemised work space. Everything has its place and can be found easily. Having clutter around will increase activity in the mind and can increase anxiety levels unnecessarily. I have found that when people are overwhelmed, feeling that they can't get things done or there's too much to do, they are often surrounded by clutter. Everything that they are working on is no doubt important, however, the brain doesn't perform at its optimum when there is an overload of inputs.

For example:

You may have a file out while working on contracts for a client. At the same time, you have another out where you are writing advertising copy. A third file is on your desk that you'll need to chase building reports.

The problem here is that if your eyes can see the files, your brain will be constantly switching from one file to the next, often at a rate so fast, you don't even know it's happening. The part of your brain that is required to do this thinking is so small, it can get overloaded very quickly. Having all these files in sight in no order will increase stress levels and take energy away from high level, quality thinking. You won't realise it but you are wasting physical energy through overloading your brain unnecessarily by simply having too much clutter in front of you.

There are some great books about getting organised such as *Work Smarter Not Harder* by Jack Collis and Cyril Peupion's *Work Smarter: Live Better, Getting Things Done* written by David Allen and many more.

Here are some simple rules that you can put into place immediately that will clear up your workplace:

Get rid of the clutter

When was the last time you had a good clean out? If you have piles of paperwork on your desk, chances are you don't know what is even there. Start by separating your desk into five places. Get every piece of paper work and put it into one pile then begin to separate it as follows:

1. *Do today*

This is what you want to complete *today*. It can be used as an in-tray but must be sorted out every day. At the end of each day, this tray should be empty.

2. *Delegate*

This pile is what you need others to do.

3. *Resources* (including reading materials such as journals, newsletters etc)

This is a place where you want to keep reading material for future reference or to read. This is where you can keep resources for times when you have some free time to catch up, or want to do some low level thinking activity to take a mental break.

4. *Waiting*

This is where you are waiting on others so you can complete a task. You may be waiting on a quote for advertising or a client has to sign some documentation. This pile must be reviewed once a day to see if anything has changed.

5. Rubbish

If you no longer need it or it has been sitting around and you don't need it in the future, get rid of it. You have to be brutal here or you will end up with a pile of stuff you will never look at again.

Depending on how much clutter you are surrounded by, this process should be completed over a few hours at the most. You should be left with a clean desk with trays appropriately labelled that are easily accessible but aren't distracting you throughout the day.

Computer files

Treat your electronic files the same way you do your paper files. Create files in different areas and keep a simple system. So much time can be wasted looking for past records because of poorly organised computer files.

Database

Most agents will have some access to a database. There was a time when we used to gauge the value of the database based on its size. Modern thinking is that the quality of the data is much more important that the size. Of course, a large high quality database is best. Keeping good quality data, that is easily accessible, will support the high performance agent. The less time it takes to retrieve the data and the higher the quality, the less effort is required to extract what is needed. Using less energy here will allow the high performer to spend their energy using the data in dollar productive activities.

Email

Email is one of the biggest distractions in today's modern workplace. Many studies show that email can actually slow productivity down, even though we feel like it improves productivity. Email itself is an amazing resource and can be used to enhance productivity and performance, provided it is used correctly.

Checking email

Limit yourself to checking you messages every one to two hours only. Many suggest that this should be only once or twice per day, however you may not find that to be sufficient. Check your mail first thing to ensure there is nothing pressing or of an urgent nature. If there is nothing that needs to be actioned immediately, change your screen so you can't see your emails sitting there while you work. Like having files laying around, seeing emails in front of you will create unnecessary distractions and can draw you away from high dollar productive tasks. Understand that you have to be able to decide very quickly where something needs to be actioned and when.

Create folders within your email like you have with your physical files. Name them 'today', 'waiting on replies or information', 'resources' and 'for reading later'. Delete the rest.

Be mindful that because it is someone else's priority, it doesn't mean it is yours. Every time you move away from what you need to get done, you are extending the time it will take to become a high performer.

Phones

The ability to be available anywhere at any time can be a great benefit to agents. No longer do you need to be pinned to the desk just in case a call comes in. Like email, used well, our phones can give great freedom in massively increased productivity, however it can also get in the way of becoming a high performer. Like computers and email, the phone can become a distraction in getting things done. You may be hard at work in high dollar activities and a phone call can ruin that in seconds. When trying to complete a task, turn the phone off or divert it to messages. If using the phone for outbound calls, restrict inbound calls until you are ready to receive calls again.

Your diary

There are so many options today when it comes to getting organised. From the old-fashioned paper diary and note books to high technology like BlackBerrys, iPhones, and iPads, just to name a few. It is more important to choose the option that works for you, versus what you think you should use. Having a well-planned diary is the basis of getting organised and streamlining your days and weeks. The more forward planning you do, the less thinking you will need to do, so you can save the thinking for other areas of your day. Whether you are using a paper or electronic diary, the same rules apply to getting organised:

1. Arranging your diary

Go though the whole calendar year and put in all your reoccurring appointments. These may include meetings, days off, lunch breaks etc. Anything that is done over and over either daily, weekly or monthly. These are usually appointments with either yourself or others that never or rarely change. The benefit in using an electronic diary is if you are using Outlook, you can set a reoccurring appointment automatically. The key is that regardless of how important the appointment is, record it in your diary. This should include all appointments with yourself such as gym, lunch, start and finish times, holidays and weekends off.

2. Block out all dollar productive time

The most important part of a high performer's day is to spend time in high dollar productive tasks. These include all prospecting activities and time for planning and follow up appointments. This is probably one of the most neglected activities to block out, however, it is one of the most important. Because some of these tasks can be challenging and require effort, it's often easier to bump them to another time or day. Having dollar productive activities blocked out in your diary will help you stay focused on what you need to get done, as well as stop you from getting to the end of the day without completing your money-making tasks.

3. Plan for chaos

One of the biggest mistakes I see people making when they decide to arrange their diaries is that they don't allow for anything to go wrong. Unfortunately, from time to time, no matter how good your intentions are and how much planning you do, things come up that throw you off track. Sometimes tasks that you plan for can run over time. This may be out of your control. Allow time in your diary to have some flexibility. If you plan every minute of every day, it is likely not to work, you will find yourself not working to your daily tasks and will eventually give up on it altogether. As a rule, look at planning between sixty to eighty per cent of your day and allow space around this for unexpected changes and over runs in time. Having your week set out will also allow you, if needed, to reschedule appointments with yourself or others. You can easily move appointments not completed to the flexible space in another time slot or day.

Mental preparation

Taking control of your physical space is a fairly simple concept to understand and a widely understood way of getting organised for high productivity. However, preparing ourselves mentally for high performance is less understood. For decades, it has been well understood how important it is for athletes to prepare mentally for high performance. It is widely recognised that it is the mental preparation and mind control that sets the best athletes in the world apart from the others.

The past ten years have seen a dramatic increase in the studies done in the field of Neuroscience in the workplace and how it affects performance. By understanding the impact of how the brain works, we can start to use this to our advantage in the workplace and everyday lives.

Like taking control of our physical workspace, we need to also become mindful of how our thinking affects what we do every day of our lives. And like the elite athletes, what we think is critical in moving us from a good agent to a high performing agent.

Healthy mind start

We all know how important it is to start the day with a healthy, nutritious breakfast. It starts the metabolism going and gets us functioning, ready for the day ahead. Starting with a healthy breakfast also stops us from getting tired throughout the day and stops us from bingeing on unhealthy foods because we are hungry.

Starting the day with a healthy mind does for your brain's performance what breakfast does for your body. The way we start the day mentally will have a direct effect on what we get done, how we react to difficult challenges throughout the day and how we keep focused for most of the day.

When we start our day, and I mean as soon as you wake – whether you are aware of it or not – your conscious brain has already started. In fact, your brain can kick into gear even before you open your eyes. What we begin to think about as soon as we are conscious can affect your performance for the rest of the day.

Many people would think that our day starts when we get to work, and that may be true for our physical work, but not so for your mental work. How our day begins will be with a set of thoughts or conversations with yourself.

Conversations like: "Monday, only four more days," or "I've got to make ten new contacts today," or "I'm excited, I've got a day off," or "What have I got on today?" or "I'm not looking forward to this morning's meetings".

Taking immediate control of your thinking first thing in the morning will set up the rest of the day. Is the conversation you are having with yourself – the self-talk – positive or negative? Is the self-talk based on a set of assumptions or reality? What you begin to think about may not even be true, but simply a story that you've developed in your mind. However, to you it can feel as real as if it has actually already happened.

Review your goals every day

One of the best ways to take control of your thinking first thing in the morning is to revisit your goals. This will move your attention to what it is you are trying to achieve, no matter how you're feeling at the time. By reviewing your goals, it will help you focus on the tasks needed to be done today that will get you closer to what you want. Any problem that you may be preparing for will become less important as you pay attention to what you want, versus what you don't want

Set an intention for the day

Another great way to get your mind in the right place is to set an intention. By setting an intention, it will have a calming effect on your mind. Knowing what it is you are going to achieve today gives certainty to the brain, which helps relieve any stresses or anxiety, allowing the brain to focus on the important tasks ahead. Having an intention is like a mini goal within your goals. Once complete, you will have a sense of achievement that will add more brain connections to the positive habits you have used throughout the day.

Examples of an intention could be:

Acknowledge all my work colleagues today
Complete all actions within a goal
Don't allow negative self-talk in all day
Be home on time to eat with the family
Have a full hour lunch break

As you can see, the intention need not to be difficult, but giving yourself something to work towards throughout your day will prepare you mentally, ready to work at a high performance level.

Clear your mind

Having a clear mind before you begin work will prepare you for high level thinking in dollar productive activities and dramatically reduce stress levels should something go wrong in the day. Here are some mind clearing tips:

Quick mind dump

The first way to clear the mind is to get everything out. Do this by taking quick notes in dot point of the things that are sitting in your head. Ideally, this should be done the day before, however, if there are any new ideas that are pressing first thing in the morning, write them down in a safe place to come back to later.

Focus on one thing

The next way to get the mind ready for high performance is to move your attention on to one thing that requires very little thinking, such as music. Listening to your favourite music or radio show will bring your attention to one point. This will help quieten the mind and begin to free up the part of the brain that does all the thinking. Some might call this meditation. Exercise is another focusing method people might choose. Once again, moving your attention to one place, away from thinking, will help you to begin your day with great energy and low stress, ready to get straight into your high level, high performance activities.

Take control of your thinking

So now that you have created a well-organised physical space where everything has its place and you are free from clutter, your mind won't get distracted with information all over the place. However, as we go though the day, we will face challenges that will need to be overcome; some will be small, others could be rather large. The way you think about the problems as they occur will have a dramatic impact on your performance throughout the day or possibly days. Starting the day with a healthy mindset will reduce the initial impact of any problems that occur. However, what you think and how you react will also have a big impact on yourself and others.

When problems occur, a high performer will start looking for solutions immediately. Rather than dig into the problem, they will try and look at it from a higher level. They won't look to blame others or try and avoid the situation, but deal with the facts and start to solve what's gone wrong. Becoming mindful at this point of your thinking is important to your performance. This is often where the negative self-talk can start and snowball into something bigger than reality.

- "I can't believe this happened, last time it did, the deal fell over" or
- "This isn't my problem, someone else will have to fix this" or
- "I'm not cut out for this, I can't seem to get any sales"

Many people are not even aware of this type of self-talk happening. And even worse, they believe what they are saying to themselves. A high performer deals with the facts of the issue and believes that this is not a reoccurring pattern but an isolated event.

High performers recover faster

High performers have a quick recovery rate. They are able to set aside the thinking associated with the past problems quickly and refocus back on the high dollar activities. Continually analysing a situation that occurred in the past won't allow thinking that will move you forward. Understanding what happened and how it can be avoided in the future is great learning but the sooner you move on, the faster you can get on with another win. The ability to control the self-talk is a habit, and high performers have this one mastered.

In his book *Learned Optimism,* Martin Seligman PH.D discusses the effects of optimism on sales performance and how self-talk can either increase or decrease productivity. What we say to ourselves – our internal dialogue – will have a profound effect on our performance and our rate of recovery after rejection. By disputing what we say to ourselves and challenging the reality of what is true and what is not, we can begin to change. According to Dr Seligman, by listening to your internal dialogue, you can start to dispute the negative self-talk and change the dialogue to an optimistic conversation.

For example:

Prospecting for appraisals

Problem: After contacting the person several times, they weren't interested in making an appointment to discuss selling.

Self-Talk: "It wasn't fair that after all the time I spent talking with them, they changed their mind. I must have said something wrong."

Results of self-talk: I felt that I wasted all that time following up, when I could have been doing something else.

Disputation: All I can do is stay in touch and be available for when they are ready. I showed the benefits of what I have to offer over the others and if that's not going to work for them, then it's their loss not mine.

Learning: I was happy with my follow up and conversations. I can put this to the side and move on to the next sale.

Listing presentation

Problem: I've just got back to the office to discover I missed out on the new business.

Self-talk: "This is the second one I've missed this week, I'm not good enough at this."

Results of self-talk: I don't think this is going to get any better, other agents are just more experienced and it is going to take too long to get better.

Disputation: I gave it my best shot. I followed all the training I've learnt and I guess they were just looking for something else. I know that there is no one else who would have achieved a price as good as I could.

Learning: I'm getting to pitch to more and more people every week. Each time, I'm getting better. I'm feeling excited that all the training I've done is helping me become a top agent. I'll debrief with my boss and discuss other options I could have taken so that next time will be a win.

After practicing these techniques, you will start to develop the new habit of optimistic self self-talk, which will support you to recover quickly from any problems or adversity. Becoming mindful of what you are saying to yourself is critical to becoming a high performing agent.

Resting the mind

High performers understand the importance of down time, both physical and mental. Taking time out throughout the day and at the end of the day, to stop thinking, is an important factor in high performance. As the body needs a break to rest and recover from strenuous exercise to repair and get stronger, so does the brain.

When you are involved in high level thinking, large amounts of energy is used, creating that sense of tiredness you feel after a hard day's work. We know that jobs involving a lot of thinking can be as hard if not harder than physical jobs and certainly this is true for real estate sales. A high performer will spend a large part of their day prospecting for new business and looking for the next deal. This all involves a lot of thinking and is energy draining. Without short and regular breaks, you cannot sustain the momentum required to be consistent day in day out.

The high performer will schedule breaks throughout the day where they can rest their mind and stop thinking to maintain their energy levels all day. This may be in the form of a short walk, or reading a journal or going to the gym. Whatever it is you choose to do, it should involve low level thinking, not problem solving, to give the mind a rest.

The same can be said for after work. At the end of the day, the brain needs time to unwind and relax. One way of doing this is by dumping anything left over down into a safe place like a diary or note pad ready to deal with the next day. By doing this, you will help relieve the leftover stress from the day and set up the next day for a great start, moving yourself into a toward state as discussed in Chapter 2.

Your ability to get a better rest and higher quality sleep will increase, which will also add to the next day's performance.

Spending the time working on both physical and mental preparation is key to becoming a high performing agent. Having one without the other will make the task almost impossible, or certainly restrict your ability to get all the way to the top. Don't try and take all the steps at once. Implement one thing at a time and keep working at it until it becomes part of your daily habits. None of these ideas are new, and many you may have already heard of; however, without implementation and consistency, you will be destined for more of the same.

My Top 5 Lessons

1. Have a healthy diet and exercise program
2. Create a clean, organised person and work space
3. Set up every day with a clear and clean mindset
4. Stop negative self-talk
5. Give your brain time to rest

5

THE PEOPLE THAT MATTER

> *"Some people come into our lives and go quickly, some stay for a while and leave footprints in our hearts, and we are never, ever the same."*
> – author unknown

You are the sum of who you hang with

Have you ever added up the income of the five people you hang out with the most, besides family, and taken the average? Chances are it will be approximately what you currently earn. It's a very interesting observation on the influence others in our lives have on us in so many ways. I remember in the first three years of my real estate career, my team had a great competitive spirit to out-do each other when it came to sales. We were always pushing each other and celebrating the wins together. Although we worked really well as a team, we still always wanted to beat each other's numbers.

After a while, being quite successful within the office, I realised that if I wanted to continue to grow, I had to get out of my own environment and learn from others that were doing a lot better than I. This took me on a road trip for a few days visiting other great offices and talking with salespeople who were at the top of the industry at the time. Moving out of my familiar environment gave me the opportunity to not only learn from others but to also observe what I was already doing well. I never went for more than six months before I attended new training or a networking event both inside and outside the industry. Listening to other great people that I could see had a similar journey to me made me understand that if you want to be successful, you need to hang out with other successful people.

Becoming a high performing real estate agent requires a lot of discipline, energy, dedication and drive. I believe that there are two different people in your life. The ones who take energy, and the ones who give. If you spend too much time with the ones who take energy, you will be constantly drawn into their problems and drama, which will ultimately affect your performance.

Get your friends and family onboard

The real estate industry can be a high stress environment and can place a lot of pressure on relationships, including those with partners, husband and wives, children and friends. To be a high performer, you need the full support of the people around you and to know that they understand what it is you do.

If you're in a relationship that is not supportive of the work and hours required to become a high performer, you need to deal with that now. The business is constant and many after hours work is required to become a high performer. The people closest to you need to understand and accept this to enable you to perform at your best. It's equally important that attention is paid to these relationships and being fully present to that relationship is your responsibility.

A high performer understands that when time is allocated to friends and family, such as weekends off and holidays, they must be completely present and give their full attention to the people around them at that time. Turn off the phone when you're not required so that you're not constantly interrupted.

A high performer doesn't make themselves available to everyone all the time. They are very clear as to when they will take calls from clients and from which clients.

Openly encourage discussions around any problems as they occur that may have an effect on the relationships. The sooner issues are dealt with, the sooner you can get on and perform at your best. It is not possible to consistently perform at a high level if there are personal issues lingering in the back of your mind. It will become a distraction and either consciously or unconsciously affect all aspects of your career.

There have been many amazing real estate careers destroyed through lack of understanding from both the agent and their families. Learning to create great balance is the key to longevity and consistency – and having all your family and friends onboard is critical to success.

Surround yourself with high performers

All top performers, regardless of whether they are managers, athletes or musicians, surround themselves with like-minded people. This maybe in a physical sense, like having a coach or surrounding themselves with resources such as books and training videos. High performers are constant learners and know that not only do they need to keep up with the latest trends and training but also know there is always something new to learn.

To be a high performer, you will need a coach. Just like the world's number one tennis player, they keep using a coach. At no time do they say to themselves:

"I'm better than everyone else, I don't need any more coaching."

The same can be said for real estate top performers. They use coaches to improve what they are already are good at, learn new and more efficient ways of doing things and bounce thoughts and ideas off them. They are never afraid to ask questions and be challenged by their coaches to stretch beyond their current thinking. High performers have mentors. People who understand what they do and can support them through any challenges they may have. The mentors may not be in real estate, but they have significant experience in certain fields that can benefit them in different aspects of their careers and life.

There are many different options when selecting a coach or mentor with different costs associated with each of them. My experience has been you get what you pay for. If you're going to engage a coach, start by asking around to see who might be best suited to you. Spend the time to shortlist and interview them, being really clear about what it is you want from them. It's a big expense, so take your time and be sure to talk to plenty of their past clients first.

However, in your journey to becoming a high performer, funds may be tight at first, so you need to be resourceful when looking for coaching. Try doing a Google search for free real estate resources or YouTube. Hundreds of beneficial free options and resources can be found on the internet. Talk with others in the office that have had more years' experience than you; they will be more than happy to help you out. A word of caution, however. As well-meaning as they may be, be careful not to fall into believing everything they say. Take on what's going to support your journey to the top, and leave all the rest.

Who's holding you back?

As you begin to grow as an agent and start to change your negative habits to become a high performer, some people in your life will not want you to change. They may be very well-meaning, however, true friends and supportive colleagues will want to see you grow and succeed. There will be people in your life right now that you probably avoid because they only want to talk about what's wrong or what's not going well. There is nothing to gain from hanging out with these people and plenty to lose. If they are someone that's important to you, it's time you had a conversation with them to explain the type of relationship you want. If after several attempts to move the conversation to something positive nothing changes, then it's time they go. Sure, from time to time people may genuinely need your help and I'm not saying walk away from them, however, at some point after everything you have done and there is nothing left to do, it's time they started helping themselves.

Disruptive work environment

Unfortunately, in a work environment it's not so easy to get rid of the negative influences around you. If the environment that you work in is completely out of line with your principles and values and you see no future there, leave. If the underlying business is the type of environment you want to work in, then it is you that will need to make some changes. As a coach, I understand that for people to change, they need to want to change. They also need to change for themselves. No matter how hard you may try to get people thinking your way, it's highly unlikely they will. So if you are faced with having to work with people that don't support you and what you want, you need to implement strategies and actions that will support you.

For example:

You work in a great office, however, there are a few people who seem to constantly interrupt you when you are trying to make your calls.
- Talk directly to the people in private and let them know that although what they have to say is interesting, it's disruptive when you're trying to make calls. Perhaps they could wait until breaks throughout the day? Understand that you have made a decision to become a high performer and that requires some significant changes. If you don't share this with others, they won't

understand. You will find that most people will respect your commitment and support what you're trying to achieve.
- Discuss it with your manager or boss and explain what it is you're trying to achieve. They too will help support you by perhaps discussing it in sales meetings. After all, what you're going to do will benefit everyone else.
- Think about when you make the calls. Can they be made at a time when there are less distractions from others? Perhaps call later in the day or earlier in the morning?
- If you are in a noisy open-plan office, find a quiet place to make the calls. Perhaps in a meeting room or spare office? If that's not available, then perhaps in your car or even at home if your office will allow.

The main point here is that you can always find someone else to blame for not doing what you know you should. Keep looking for a solution until you're satisfied you can get the job done.

My Top 5 Lessons

1. **The people around you will have an effect on your performance**
2. **Make sure all your family and friends understand the journey you're about to take**
3. **Surround yourself with people whom you who like to emulate**
4. **Get rid of the negative people in your life**
5. **Take responsibility to create the changes you need to perform at a high level. Others won't change – you need to**

6

REAL ESTATE WITH THE BRAIN IN MIND

"A man's mind once stretched by a new idea, never regains its original dimensions."
– Oliver Wendell Holmes

Now that we understand why both physical and mental preparation are so critical to ensure the success of high performing agents, I want to look at the most critical aspect of real estate – prospecting – and how understanding the brain better will increase performance dramatically and thus increase success.

To perform at a consistent and high level, we need to be in a positive mind frame or a toward mental state. This is also essential in order to perform the high level thinking that's necessary when having conversations around prospecting and searching for new business.

As discussed in earlier chapters, our natural brain state has a tendency towards slight anxiousness, or fear, before we even start the day. This may be heightened, depending on what else is going on at the time. If you have just walked out the door to jump into your car to discover that your tyres are flat, you will be pushed even further into this natural away state. Or perhaps you slept in and are now running late for an important meeting. Just the smallest thing can lead us into a greater state of anxiousness, which will flow into our working day if we allow it.

Prospecting

Prospecting is the number one key skill to building a successful real estate career. A great deal of time is spent by trainers around this area of the business, as it is vital when building a new real estate career and equally critical to maintain momentum and consistency throughout a career. It's also the area that is most resisted by real estate agents and the greatest source of frustration by managers and bosses is getting their sales people to prospect consistently.

But why do we resist prospecting and how can we overcome it?

Problem 1 – Fear

Fear of rejection is the number one biggest reason prospecting is either done inconsistently or not done at all. This is true for most sales careers and once you have the ability to overcome the fear, your real estate career will boom.

Prospecting or looking for new business requires talking with people who we may have never met before or have a limited relationship with. Because our default state of being is to be wary of new things, as a survival mechanism, we will naturally have a sense of fear or anxiety. When we make prospecting calls, we can fear that the other person may not want to talk with us or not know who we are. Thinking this way moves us into a fear state.

Solution 1 – Begin in a positive mental state

Start your call sessions in a toward state of mind. Moving in this direction will lower anxiety levels and lessen any fears you will have. You can do this by avoiding situations that put you in a natural state of fear, for example running late for appointments or checking emails or messages that may contain problems that need your attention. Avoid conversations with others that may affect your thinking in a negative sense prior to making the calls.

Solution 2 – Stop thinking

This is perhaps harder than it may seem. However, one of the main reasons why we move into an away state mentally is our negative thinking or self-talk. Given that you are yet to do the calls, any thoughts around what may happen are simple assumptions about the future and aren't real. Knowing this, any negative self-talk will only add to the way you feel. Using methods to stop the thinking will support your mental preparation. Listening to music or exercising will help you focus on something else, thereby limiting or stopping the negative thinking. It's not important what you do to limit or stop the thinking, as long as it moves your thinking away from creating negative self-talk.

Solution 3 – Change the self-talk

If we know our natural tendency is towards fear, the more negative thoughts we allow in, the more we will add to the fear state. Re-appraising our thinking or changing the way we think about the situation will move us to a toward state, allowing positive and clear thinking to come in. Changing the way we see the future in our thinking will shift your mind from a negative fear state towards a positive state.

Example:

Negative self-talk

"When I called these people last time, they said they aren't ready to sell. So If I call them again, they will probably get annoyed and be short with me on the phone. They will probably think I am just being pushy and ask me not to call them again."

Reappraise the conversation

"Last time I called them, they weren't ready to sell. However, they are probably curious as to how things are selling at present and what recent sales there may have been that are similar to theirs. If I can give them as much information as possible, it will help them to make the best choices when it comes to selling. They will see me as someone they can trust that is knowledgeable and hopefully call on me when they're ready to sell in the future."

Negative self-talk

"They told me they would contact me when they were ready to sell, so there is no need to call them. If I do call them, they will probably get annoyed and ask me not to call again."

Reappraise the conversation

"They told me they would call when they were ready to sell. However, I'm sure they would want to know about the sale that has just happened down the road from them. They will appreciate the fact that I'm keeping them informed of the market conditions and, at the same time, I'm showing them I'm fully informed about the market. When the time comes and they decide to sell, they will remember me keeping them updated. Every time I make another call, it increases my opportunities to list another house, which is critical to achieving my goals."

When it comes to the way you think, you have a choice to allow thoughts that support high quality focused prospecting or negative self-talk that will hold you back. To become a high performing agent, you need to move past the fear that is holding you back and move your thinking to a place that supports the positive actions that will consistently generate appraisals.

Problem 2 – Lack of planning

One of our greatest fears as humans is the unknown. Not knowing what is about to happen either now or in the future will create anxiety and fear. If we approach prospecting from an ad hoc position, not knowing what we are about to do will increase this fear and reduce the ability to think clearly and stay focused. The brain likes organisation and structure, and having a clear idea of the sort of prospecting you want to do, when you want to do it and for how long will provide certainty to the brain and reduce fear and anxiety.

Steps to help with your planning

1. Block out the time in advance in your diary. Work to a maximum of one hour blocks before taking a break for 15 minutes.

2. Get the prospecting done first thing in the morning. Our energy levels are at their highest in the morning and there is less chance of being distracted with other events from the day. Getting it done and out of the way early will provide a great sense of satisfaction, which will support this habit.

3. Don't mix up your calls. Do blocks of similar type calls (ie. past appraisals or clients, or pasts buyers or anniversary calls, for example). Keeping the conversation the same will not only help hone the dialogue but it will also reduce what you need to think about during the conversation, giving the brain time to rest. With each call on the same topic, the conversation gets easier, which helps reduce fear and grow the positive prospecting habit.

4. Work from a written list. Agents will often work straight out of their database, filling in details as they go. This may work for some, however, both from a time point of view and with the brain in mind, it is not efficient. Working from a written list and leaving filling out details until later keeps the mind focused on one thing at a time. Every time you shift from one task to another, your brain needs to switch from one thinking to another albeit very rapidly. This will use more physical energy and create the chance to

be easily distracted. Reducing the processes needed for a task will help the thinking stay at a high level and focused.

Problem 3 – Lack of commitment

No matter how much we may want something, unless we are committed to it, it will forever stay out of reach. Prospecting can be a grind and you can suffer rejection repeatedly. Unless you are committed to the end result, you are likely to underperform or fail. The problem is that becoming committed to doing prospecting isn't very exciting for most people; after all, it's challenging and can take a long time without seeing any real results. So how do you make a commitment to prospect constantly?

Solution 1 – Set targets

Selling homes is a numbers game. The more people you speak with, the more chance you have of getting appraisals. More appraisals increase your chances of more listings. More listings means more sales. The more sales you do, the more evidence of your success and the more people will want to deal with you. The more people want to deal with you, the more appraisals you get and the cycle continues. If you track your numbers, even when the results aren't immediate, you can be assured that you will begin to hit targets.

For example:

If you know that for every call you make to past appraisals, you will get one out of ten to list, you know that after making 100 calls you will get ten chances to list. Of course, there will be variations to these numbers based on who you are calling and how long you have had the relationship for but, eventually, you will start to see a pattern.

Targets can be set in many areas. However, some prospecting key performance indicators or KPIs that should be tracked include:

- Number of outbound calls
- Number of connections made
- Number of direct mail sent
- Number of listing opportunities
- Number of listings gained
- Number of doors knocked
- Number of conversion of door knocks to appraisals

As a general rule, if you do a task that is repeated daily, weekly or monthly that counts as prospecting, measure the KPI. Having a measure will keep you focused on what is working, what needs to improve and this in itself will create organisation for your brain. You will have a greater sense of calm, even when you're not achieving the sales you would like. You will know that you are committed to the numbers and eventually the sales will flow.

- Solution 2 – Set goals

As discussed earlier, KPIs or targets are not goals. They are simply numbers we count that, if done consistently, will eventuate in results. The problem with targets is that they are not very exciting and inspiring, and even the most dedicated agent will eventually find that just working towards achieving the KPIs will not be enough and the commitment to continue will be low at best.

Setting goals lifts your thinking from the now to the future, pulling you out from minor details, problems and drama to see a clear vision of what you want. As the brain likes certainty, looking three, six or twelve months out and knowing what it is you want will help with any day-to-day anxiousness that may come with prospecting. Having something in the future to look towards, makes doing difficult tasks a lot easier. You know there's a light at the end of the tunnel.

An example of this is when we are getting ready to have a holiday. We have a deadline to work towards, we know that we need to get certain things done before we go so we can relax, and everything that was difficult or hard seems a little easier because there is a reward at the end. We are less distracted by others and things that aren't important to getting the job done, before the holidays. A goal in the future serves the same purpose. Having something inspiring and exciting that stands above the day-to-day tasks will allow you to bounce back from rejection easier and help you move on to the next task quicker.

If your goal is to finish saving towards a deposit on a house, you know that with every call and every contact you are moving closer to achieving that goal. You are committed to something much greater than just prospecting. There is purpose in what you are doing and with every win, you build the positive habit of prospecting, which will get easier every time. The easier it becomes, the more you can do and the faster the results. The faster the results, the faster you will get to achieving your goal.

My Top 5 Lessons

1. Get into a positive mental space
2. Don't allow negative thinking in
3. Plan your prospecting in advance
4. Work towards targets and key performance indicators
5. Set short and long-term goals

7

HIGH PERFORMANCE TEAMS

"Coming together is the beginning, keeping together is progress, working together is success."
– author unknown

While I was writing this book, I had the privilege to work with a great real estate team over a ten-week period. We established a goal that the team was excited about and set about planning our strategies and actions to achieve that goal. Feelings were mixed among the group about what was going to happen over the coming weeks. There was some excitement, some scepticism and plenty of curiosity. However, everyone was onboard to give it a go. As we worked through the session, the feelings from the team changed regularly; however, they were committed to their goal and continued with the strategies and actions they needed to succeed.

By the time the ten sessions were complete, not only had they exceeded their goal, it was clear there had been a positive and permanent change within the team. Their learning went far beyond just achieving their goals, they learnt more about themselves and each other, than they ever knew before. From the sessions, they became much more focused on the things that are important to them achieving their goals in real estate and their private lives. They became a much tighter team, supporting and respecting each other on a whole new level. The new positive habits they have learnt will serve them well into the future, no matter where they want their careers to go.

The main difference with creating high performing teams versus a high performing individual is that there is a common vision and goal that is shared by all. As salespeople in a real estate office, each individual is essentially a business within themselves and will have their own key performance indicators and goals to work towards. However, most salespeople work with others trying to do the same things and, if they aren't aligned under a common goal, it makes it difficult for the whole team to perform.

For example:

If there is an individual trying to focus on making prospecting calls but they are interrupted constantly by office chatter, it will reduce the performance of the individual and create frustration and sometimes resentment. Without the alignment of a common goal, there will be very little consistency in the team's performance.

Groups versus teams

Perry Zeus and Suzanne Skiffington's book, *The Wisdom of Teams* distinguishes between Groups and Teams. Groups are generally not performance focused and can simply have an understanding of things in common, like a book club or walking club. A team, however, is focused on performance working towards a common goal.

Team basics include:

- Small number
- Complementary skills
- A common purpose
- A common set of performance goals
- Commonly agreed working approach
- Mutual accountability

The single most powerful engine for teams is a clear and compelling performance challenge. Research shows that the team leader is seldom the primary determinant of team performance.

In *Coaching at Work*, authors Perry Zeus and Suzanne Skiffington note that there are common factors that apply to all high performing teams, which include:

- Common purpose – a clear course and sense of direction provide context and guide the team's actions.
- Clear and specific goals – have an action plan in place and strategies to achieve the goals.
- Each member understands and is competent in his or her position – members have complementary skills such as technical expertise, decision-making skills and good interpersonal skills.
- Open communication channels – information and learning is shared among team members. Communcation is timely, clear and focused on the strategic goals of the organisation.
- Members encourage and support each other.
- Flexibility – able to rotate members to other positions, sharing or shifting of leadership roles.

- Know and utilise each member's strengths and know their weaknesses.
- Mutual accountability for team results, share the glory, do not apportion blame when things go wrong. Team members can also work as a team apart, and can con tribute to a sequence of activities rather than a common task that requires their presence in one place at the one time.
- Consistency – members can work and perform to their potential on a consistent basis.

Potential obstacles teams can face include:

- Goals and expectations
- Roles
- Systems and procedures
- Interpersonal issues

Goals and expectations:

- Unclear or no goals
- Unrealistic goals
- Out of step with team members' values/other roles

Roles:

- Lack of clarity over roles within the team and in the organisation as a whole.

Systems and procedures:

- Lack of consensus about how to achieve a goal
- Organisational systems may not support what the team is trying to achieve

Interpersonal issues:

- Fear of change
- Internal competition
- Hidden agendas, territorial struggles, mistrust
- Group dynamics

Principles of working with teams

Let them do the thinking

The role of the team leader is to help facilitate the team's thinking by helping them to think more productively and effectively than they would without the leader. However, it is the team doing the thinking, not the leader. As a leader, you are wanting to harness the collective thinking from the team, rather than push your own agenda or views. The leader must be open to listen to the group and be prepared to take on new thinking. Simply just listening then trying to convince others of your ideas will not work. Moving the conversation from telling to asking, is a great way of getting ideas out of the group.

For example:

Instead of saying...

"What we need to do is spend more time making calls and generating appointments."

You could say...

"What could we start doing this week that will help generate more appointments for the team?"

As the leader of the group, by asking questions, you will generate a collective group of ideas rather than just your own thoughts. By asking the group, you will not only get a broader range of ideas but, if they are adopted by the group, there is much more buy-in and the actions are far more likely to be completed.

Focus on solutions

It's easy to discuss the problems and shift blame around when individuals don't want to take ownership of what's not going well. Moving the conversation to solutions will keep the conversation at a planning and vision level, keeping the process moving forward. Often, when first starting work with a team, it's a great idea to put up the vision chart to keep the team focused on solutions.

VISION (Solutions focused area)
PLANNING (Solutions focused area)
DETAIL
PROBLEM
DRAMA

Each time you feel the team is moving back to discussing problems, refer back to the chart and direct their attention to Vision and Planning.

Give positive feedback

Teams need positive feedback as much as individuals. Spending time to recognise what's going well for the team is important in forming new positive habits. Look for opportunities to catch individuals and the team doing things well. Be specific and generous when it comes to feedback so they can see you are paying attention.

As stated earlier in the book, there has been a lot of research to suggest that very few organisations offer sufficient positive feedback for individuals or teams. It has been suggested that a ratio of one criticism to five positive acknowledgements is required to support positive habits and change. It's very easy when things aren't going well to point out what's not right and what's not working. However, this is the time to really focus on the things that are being done well and acknowledge them as they occur.

Make them stretch

A team with a stretch goal will make them work together, which will help create a bond within the team. They will encourage and support each other for the benefit of the team – and challenge and support one another as they share the wins.

Set the stage

Keeping the team on track can be difficult at times and it can be easy to have the conversation go all over the place. Before each team meeting, be clear about what is going to happen and the rules for how the meeting will run. This may include:

- How long the session will run
- Reviewing the goal and how the team feels about it
- What the session is about (setting new actions, brainstorming, current challenges)
- What are the outcomes for the meeting? (one new action, extra research)
- No speaking over each other
- Respect everyone's ideas
- Everyone's role in the session
- Clarifying all the important ideas

One of the most important roles of the leader is to bring all the discussion to a point where actions can be set. Clarifying the discussion helps solidify the team's ideas, so everyone agrees on what is being said and what the next steps are. It brings a set of thoughts and ideas to the bottom line and encourages discussion that will generate new ideas for the team.

Establish a common goal for the team

Like individuals, teams must have a goal to work towards to keep focused and thinking at a high level. Most real estate offices operate with individuals on targets that are combined with other salespeople to make up the office targets. Salespeople and their managers see themselves as businesses within another business, which to a degree is true. However, the challenge is how to combine a group of people together with different skill sets, goals, needs and wants for a common purpose. By aligning the group together with a common goal, it shifts the focus from the individuals to the team. Although the individuals' performance is still critical to the team, there is a higher purpose that the team is working towards. With this common purpose, the team will become much closer as a group, supporting one another and encouraging one another through challenges. They will share the wins of the group and recognise strengths in each other that they haven't seen before. It will help create an equal footing for the individuals in the group, with the quieter ones having a greater opportunity to have a say and the louder ones less opportunity to take control of the meetings.

The key to establishing a common goal for the team is that the 'Team' must establish the goal, not the boss or sales manager. Sure, it must be aligned with the outcomes of the organisation and be beneficial to the organisation but, unless the 'Team' creates the goal, it is unlikely to succeed. If the team creates the goal, there is a much higher chance of 'buy-in'. Because they have established the goal themselves, they become attached to the process and the outcome. For an individual goal to be successful, it must be inspiring and exciting. The same must be said for the team. Using the same process as you do setting individual goals, the team can begin to establish a common goal. It must have a measure so they know when they have succeeded.

For example:

Team sales goals

"We are number one (goal), we have market share." (measure)

"We have succeeded (goal), our listings have doubled." (measure)

Whatever the goal, it is important to keep working until everyone is onboard. Keep checking in with the group and clarifying that you are moving towards a goal that is inspiring to all. Remember it must be achievable, a stretch and written clearly. Once the goal has been established, continue to work through the processes of developing strategies and actions. When working with teams, be sure to share actions among the group and give everyone equal say. Allow time for those who don't speak up as often – and make sure everyone stays onboard. Review the actions after completion and check in on how well the team is going. Acknowledge what's not going well but stay focused on what is going well, and don't dwell on problems and drama. Be sure to celebrate the wins along the way, no matter how small, and spend plenty of time acknowledging the team and the individuals as they have successes.

NOTES

PART 2

THE PERFECT DAY

This is Chris's story. A high performing agent, he has learnt what it takes to be at the top of his game. He is guided by his habits, however, his habits are those of the elite few. Follow Chris through his day and observe what he does to be one of the best agents imaginable. You will learn what is going on in his brain that is different to other agents – and how you can apply his knowledge and habits to accelerate and enhance your career immediately.

Chapter 1 – Monday 6am–7:30am

It was a bitterly cold morning when the screech of the alarm went off. Leaning over to turn it off, Chris began to think that he could go for a walk this afternoon. It was so cold and he just wanted a few more minutes in bed. Chris had been out with his mates over the weekend and was absolutely exhausted. He noticed, however, that the last few times he tried to do this the walk never happened because he had appointments come up at the last minute and by the time he got home, it was too late and he was too exhausted.

Without another thought, he rolled the sheets off the bed,

sat up and went straight over to get dressed. He slipped on his shoes grabbed is iPod and within a few minutes, he was dressed and ready to set off on his walk. Chris enjoyed this time as it gave him an opportunity to contemplate what he wanted to achieve today. He knew that he had a set of tasks to perform that were set up in his calendar, jobs that he completed every Monday. He had a couple of great leads to chase today that came in over the weekend that could turn into new listings. However, a deal he'd been working on for some time looked like it might fall over due to significant structural issues that came out in a building report.

The sale had been a challenge all along, the vendors had bought elsewhere and were getting ever more desperate to try and get a sale. Chris had provided great service and advice the whole way along, however, the owners were getting anxious and increasingly agitated as they were under financial pressure to get the sale done as quickly as possible. He knew that this extra problem wouldn't sit well with the owner and he was worried about how they would react. He started to hear the story in his head "Oh my god! We can't afford to lose this sale!" "What else can go wrong?" "We are never going to sell this home," and "I told you to make sure there were not going to be any problems! "

The conversation could go in many directions, however, Chris knew he had seen these situations before and was confident that he could work with both seller and buyer to overcome the issue. After all, it was out of his control, he could only offer options to both sides, to try to resolve the issue.

He popped in his head phones and dialled up this favourite music as he started to warm up. The day was turning out great, the sun was shining and he finally had warmed up, what a great way to start the day, he said to himself. As he walked through the streets, he took notice of what was around him, acknowledging others that were out walking and running. After another ten minutes, he found himself thinking about the problem sale again and decided to move his thoughts and attention to an upcoming holiday he had planned. In two weeks' time, Chris was heading off overseas for a well-earned break for some R&R. He pictured himself lying by the pool warming himself in the sun. It suddenly dawned on him that he still hadn't arranged his passports and it was something that needed to be done. He reached into his pocket and grabbed his phone and made a voice mail note to follow it up later that day.

Soon Chris was back home from his walk feeling great, he was pleased he had made the effort to get out of bed on this freezing morning. He had great energy and was looking forward to the rest of the day. After a quick shower and change, he sat and enjoyed his breakfast at the table. He started to move his thinking to what was ahead at work. He knew Mondays were busy days catching up on the weekend and all the inspections he had done. Chris also scheduled all his calls to his owners to catch them up on the weekend activity. Mondays were a great day to prospect for new business with all the open house calls he has to make. They were a great source of new business for him, and it was something he always looked forward to. He went over the dialogue he uses on the phone in his head so he was really clear about what he wanted to achieve through those calls.

Monday was also a day he chose a street to cold call, looking for new business. His success had been patchy, however he knew it was about the numbers. The more 'nos' he got, the closer he got to a 'yes'. He knew that for him to achieve his goals, this was a critical part of his week. Chris finished off his breakfast, grabbed his briefcase, jumped in the car and headed off to work.

Thinking about Chapter 1

When Chris woke up, he knew it was his normal morning to walk but he still considered not going. His old habits of lying in bed till the last minute are still present, something he'd been doing for years. Chris had been walking now for six months, so walking was his new habit. Even so, it wasn't easy and he had to remind himself how much better he feels for it. Chris knew from past experience that the best thing to do was to not think, so he just got up and started to move without further thought. He could also relax knowing that once his walk was out of the way, he didn't have to take up valuable thinking time throughout the day wondering if his afternoon walk would happen. Chris also knew that starting the day with some exercise gave him more energy throughout the day, particularly if challenges were to come up requiring him to do some problem solving.

By having all his clothes laid out, he didn't have to think about what to do next. He would just go on autopilot and get started. The brain likes to take the easiest path. By not having to think about what he needed to do to get ready first thing in the morning, his chances of going for his walk are much better. There is also less chance of lying in bed finding another excuse not to walk. "I don't know where my runners are" or "I'm just not organised". There was nothing to do but just get up and go.

As Chris began to walk, he started to think about what's ahead for him during the day. Because Chris has a well-organised diary, he knows all the information he needs for the day is in a safe place and he doesn't have to think about it anymore. Knowing that he is well-organised lowers any anxiety he may have and starts him in a toward state within the brain. This is where Chris's brain works best when he needs do some high level thinking throughout the day. He has cold calling to do and moving in a towards state mentally, he will be better prepared.

As Chris continued to walk, he started thinking about a problem that he was going to face for the day, a bad result on a building inspection. His natural tendency was to start thinking about how the situation may play out in a bad way. However, Chris knew that thinking this way would only raise his anxiety levels and affect him for the rest of the day. Instead, he acknowledged what was going on for him, told himself he had the skills to handle the situation and put it out of his mind.

As he popped his headphones on, he drew his attention to the music and removed any thoughts about work. He started noticing what was going around him, which further drew his attention away from any thoughts that may inhibit his high level thinking for later that day. When he started thinking about his upcoming holiday, he realised that he hadn't checked his passport. Rather than trying to keep the thought in his head, which would require him to keep thinking about it until he had it done it and not forgotten, his organisation habits came forward, so he moved the thought into a safe place in the form of a voice note on his phone. As Chris ate breakfast, he purposely moved his attention to what his intentions are for the day. Making vendor calls and his pre-arranged cold calls. Doing this started him focusing on the results he wanted for the day. Chris had some great goals and a part of achieving these was to continue to prospect consistently. He didn't like cold calling but he knew that it was just part of what he needed to do to succeed in his goals. Chris had set himself up for a great day. He is relaxed and focused, well-organised and ready for any challenges that may appear throughout the day.

Chapter 2 – Monday 7:30am–8:15am

Well-organised and feeling relaxed, Chris sets off for work. It is about a 30-minute drive, so he uses the time to make a few client calls, catching up with people that refer him a lot of business. Many of Chris's clients start early, so he likes to get these calls done before he gets to work. During one of these calls, one of his clients, John, says he had heard a property around the corner from him may be coming on the market. Chris thanks John for the lead and stops to take some notes. He's now about five minutes away from work, so Chris pops on his favourite music, turns off his phone and enjoys the last few minutes' drive.

Thinking about Chapter 2

Chris knows that staying in touch with his past clients is one of the most important habits he has in building his business. Calling people he knows doesn't create any unnecessary anxiety that may affect him throughout the day, and often helps him get even better prepared for the more difficult calls when he gets to work. Chris feels a sense of achievement, having already begun his prospecting for the day. Unknowingly, he acknowledges himself for his discipline in making the calls, something he does most days. Acknowledging himself helps to build the positive habit of making these client calls. Each time he makes these calls, he keeps building on this habit, which is part of his success as a high performing agent.

Chapter 3 – Monday 8:15am–12pm

Arriving at work, Chris moves straight to his desk, saying a quick hello to the other people in the office and boots up his computer. He knows he has a few calls to make and the problem with the building inspection that must be dealt with. He makes some quick notes about what he needs to get done and gets on with his first task of the day, vendor calls. It is 8:15am and Chris works his way through his calls, updating his owners on activity over the weekend and what is happening for them over the next seven days. He works from top to bottom from his vendor list, keeping his conversations short and to the point. Carrying 15 properties at this time, he allocates about three minutes per call, finishing up before 9am.

Having finished his calls, he takes a quick break to grab a coffee and check his emails from the weekend. Scanning down the list, some great enquiries have come in and he is keen to follow them up. He notices as well a copy of the building report from the weekend that he requested so he could discuss it with his owners. With nothing urgent that requires his immediate attention, Chris turns off his computer screen, emails the office to advise he is unavailable for two hours and moves straight to his second prospecting activity for the day, cold calls.

Chris has allocated two 45-minute call sessions to contact owners of homes around his new listings. Having prepared the call lists last Friday, he can now work straight from the list in front of him, taking notes as he goes. He works his way from top to bottom, working off a familiar script. As his first 45-minute session ends, he feels a little disappointed that he hasn't generated any new leads. He takes a 15-minute break, then gets straight back into it. After another 45-minute call session, he has only generated one possible lead that he can work on down the track. Although feeling a bit deflated, he finishes up his calls and moves on to the next task at hand, past appraisals.

This is a call session Chris enjoys as he feels more comfortable calling people he has already meet and made a connection with. He sets about doing another 45-minute session and generates three new leads. Chris is now feeling great – he has completed all his vendor calls and found some great new prospects to work on – the day has started well.

Thinking about Chapter 3

Chris arrived at the office feeling focused, relaxed and in control. He had set himself up mentally to be in a toward state with his activities so far. Arriving at the office, Chris knew exactly what he was going to do. The brain likes certainty and feeling safe. Knowing what was ahead of him kept him calm and feeling good about the activities before him. He made a point of not getting involved in the office chat, which sounded interesting but he was focused on the important tasks of the day – vendor calls, cold calls and past appraisals. Calling his vendors first gets this out of the way from both a practical sense and a mental sense as it clears his mind of this task. He knows that his owners are going to want to be updated and if he doesn't do it now, he may run out of time and they may start to call him. Taking control of this process keeps his day on schedule, rather than having outside influences or other people affecting his routine. The part of the brain where all the good quality thinking is done, has a limited capacity to store thoughts. The less he stores in his mind, such as thinking about calling his owners, the better he will deal with tasks that require concentration.

One of Chris's important tasks today was to report back to his owners about the poor building report. Knowing that this could distract him from his daily calls, he chose to do this after the calls were complete. He had set himself up mentally to focus on the important tasks of the day, his call sessions. Making the call to the owner of the poor building report and knowing that the call could become challenging, he knew this could affect his positive mental state. It could possibly lead to other activities that require attention that would stop him from doing his regular, important activities for the day such as his prospecting calls.

Making cold calls or other prospecting calls requires clear and focused thinking. By choosing not to engage in a difficult conversation before his calls, Chris keeps his energy high and his thinking on one thing, the calls. Doing challenging activities that require focused thinking uses physical energy. This is why we often feel more exhausted after a difficult mental day than after a day of strenuous exercise. Thinking uses energy and the more we do, the more energy we use. If we leave these important high level thinking tasks to the end of the day, our energy will be low and the chances of giving up will be much greater. There are some exceptions, where you may feel more energy in the afternoon, however, this is rarely true. Additionally, by completing these difficult tasks first up, there is a sense of achievement when complete. This supports the positive habit of having completed the tasks, making each session less challenging as time goes by.

You may have noticed that Chris didn't spend any time replying to emails or reading any unnecessary details. Once again, this is a very simple distraction that can lead to lost productivity and loss of focus. Knowing that there weren't any urgent matters arriving in his inbox after a quick scan, turning off his computer screen stops any chance of getting distracted by incoming emails or other tasks set for the day. He knows all the information is in a safe place (emails and tasks) so there is no need to use any thinking to remember what needs to be done. He'll come back to the emails later in the day.

One of Chris's critical habits for being a high performing agent is his focus on planning. Chris had spent time preparing his call sheets the week before, so that when he got to work, it was ready to go. The brain takes the easiest path, and having the list ready to go requires less effort and energy to get the task done. The list also provides a sense of comfort and safety to the brain as he has a clear idea of what he is going to do. Another important factor in Chris's success is that he groups his calls together. He only calls the same group at the same time (ie. all cold calls or all past appraisals, or all vendor calls). Regardless of what calls he is going to make, they are in blocks of like calls.

Again, this provides the easiest path for the brain. There is no need to move between different scripts and switching thinking around with different conversations. As he works his way through the calls, he will also perfect his dialogue each time. Learning as he goes, he becomes better, which reinforces that positive habit of making the calls.

During the first call session, however, Chris didn't have the great results he would normally expect. However, he didn't allow a negative conversation to enter his mind. Chris could have tried to find excuses as to why his calls weren't working so well this time, and used that as a reason to stop, but he chose not to. Chris has the ability to stay focused on the bigger picture. At the beginning of the year, Chris set himself some great goals. He had always wanted to travel to Europe and he had decided that if he hit his targets this year, he would spend a month overseas in December.

Chris has pictures up in his office of the countries he wants to visit and the attractions that he has always wanted to see. Having a purpose, a goal that really excited him, helped him from moving into a negative conversation with himself. Instead, after a tough call session where he didn't feel like he had done very well, he kept his focus on the big picture, the Europe trip. He knew that no matter what happened in any single call session, provided he persisted, the effort would pay off. He gave no further thought to the session completed and moved on to the next.

After two sessions on cold calling, which he didn't enjoy much, he moved to one more session of past appraisals. Although he didn't get great results for the cold call sessions this time, Chris still felt good, knowing that this tough job was behind him. He acknowledged his achievement of getting some great work done, yet it was still early in the day.

Moving to past appraisals, which he felt much more comfortable about, he was feeling positive, relaxed and his mind was focused. He generated some great new leads out of the last session, which was partly due to his energy and enthusiasm for his work up to this point. Chris's mind was clear, he had continued to grow the positive habits of completing his prospecting calls early and he was feeling confident about achieving his exciting goal by the end of the year.

Chapter 4 – Monday 12pm–1:30pm

Chris is feeling great, having completed all his high dollar activities first thing in the morning. He switches his computer back on and again scans his emails, prioritising what needs to be done first. He knows he has two buyer appointments later that day, so prepares his information for those first. He grabs the brochures and information memorandum and drops them into his briefcase for later. Moving back to his computer, he moves his emails into his electronic task list, in order of priority.

(email task list)

- Call Mary Robert regarding 37 Smith St, 0401 082 292
- John returning your call about Albert St, 9871 2002
- Roger from Williams Solicitors called regarding Allerton Settlement
- Call Sean from real estate trainers about November workshops
- Reading – How to increase your listings in ten easy steps
- Database training in September with Rosalie Graham
- Pest and building report 14 Nova Ave, Petersham

Chris's first priority is to deal with the sale that had a bad pest and building report. After having a good look through the report, it becomes clear that things aren't as bad as first described – after all, he had seen plenty much worse than this. He takes a copy and highlights the areas of concern and gives the owners a call. As expected, the owners aren't happy and proceed to give Chris a blast, telling him they aren't going to compromise any further and they would rather keep the house than to sell it for anything less than they had already agreed. Chris knows that this is probably not possible as they have already purchased elsewhere and need this sale to buy the other property. Even though there had been no discussion regarding a price reduction, he notices that the owners have assumed this would be the case and continues to listen without interrupting.

When he feels the owners have expressed all their feelings, Chris begins to explain the details of the report. First, he acknowledges that he can understand their feeling angry and upset, and that it's to be expected. He goes on to let them know that he has come across reports like this on a regular basis and the chances are, everything should still proceed smoothly.

As the conversation continues, Chris and his owner agrees that they will get quotes for the work to be done and, if agreeable, they will go halves with the buyer as a compromise. After a 15-minute conversation, the owners feel better and have their confidence restored in Chris getting the sale done. They thank him for the hard work he has done up to this point and end the conversation.

Chris makes some notes about arranging tradespeople to get quotes later that day and then move on to his next task.

Following up his buyer enquiries over the weekend, Chris slots in another two buyer appointments later that day. His afternoon is now pretty full, and he has some great prospects to work with. Noticing that it is almost one o'clock, he prints some extra brochures for his new buyer appointments and heads out of the office for lunch.

Thinking about Chapter 4

It's now the middle of the day and Chris has completed all the high value, high thinking tasks. Working through prospecting calls requires a high level of energy and doing this first thing will ensure the energy levels stay high. He now moves back to his emails that don't require much thought at all. This gives his mind a chance to take a break and refocus on how the rest of the day will look.

Moving his emails from his inbox to a task list helps Chris to stay in a toward state mentally, as it helps arrange what needs to be done into a safe list. Once it's on a list, he doesn't need to keep remembering what he needs to do, which keeps his mind free for more important thinking like negotiation or tough conversations with owners about building reports.

Removing the emails from his inbox will also stop him from continually scanning what he needs to do. Each time he scans his emails, he moves his attention away from what he is currently doing. He has a very high chance of being distracted, which will lead to loss of time and productivity.

Chris needed to have a difficult conversation with his owners about a bad building report. Although he didn't know how the conversation would go, he knew that the best way to support the situation is for him to stay calm and in control. By being prepared for the call by highlighting the problems areas and thinking about how he has successfully handled this sort of conversation in the past, he was able to remain cool and stay professional to support his owners. As the conversation with the owners started to become heated, Chris just allowed them to talk. At this point, the owners are now in an anxious state mentally, which makes it difficult for them to think clearly and make important decisions. Allowing them to talk without buying into the problems, the owners' frustrations started to lessen, which began them moving back into a toward state mentally. Chris then went on to reassure them that what they were feeling was normal and that he had handled many situations like this before.

This gave some certainty and safety to the owners, which made them feel much better and, in doing so, they continued to relax and think more clearly about their situation.

Chris's actions leading up to this point, keeping himself in a toward, calm brain state supported him when he needed to stay in control of this situation. Because he is in control, he can provide the best advice, without any undue emotions and be the professional agent he is. At a time of high stress for the owners, Chris's calmness and control helped them to think clearly about the situation and ultimately move towards a reasonable solution to get some quotes to repair the problems in the report.

It had been a high level thinking morning for Chris with vendor calls, three 45-minute prospecting sessions and a tough conversation with an owner. He has used up a lot of energy up to this point and his capacity to think at a high level will start to diminish over the rest of the day. Chris has planned his day so that by now his high energy, high thinking tasks are out of the way. He can now take a break and give his mind a rest ready for the rest of the day.

Taking time away from the office to grab some lunch, he can rest mentally and recharge with some healthy food, rebuilding his energy levels. By the time Chris comes back to the office, he is feeling recharged, organised and set for a productive afternoon.

Chapter 5 – Monday 1:30pm–4pm

Chris has had a great day so far. He has caught up with all his owners from the weekend, held three prospecting sessions, handled a tough conversation with his owner regarding a bad building report and had buyer appointments lined up for the afternoon. Chris has a list of tasks to get through. Some were done every Monday and others were tasks that had popped up. He has organised his buyer inspections together between 2:30pm and 4:00pm this afternoon and has all the information ready to go. He can now focus on the tasks he has diarised for the day and start working on completing them.

TASKS

- ~~Call Mary Robert regarding 37 Smith St 0401-08-22923 DONE~~
- ~~John returning your call about Albert St 987-120023 DONE~~
- Roger from Williams Solicitors called regarding Allerton Settlement
- Call Sean from real estate trainers about November Workshops
- Reading – How to increase your listings in ten easy steps

- Database training in September with Rosalie Graham
- ~~Pest and Building report 14 Nova Ave Petersham DONE~~
- ~~Print Just Sold letters for the week~~
- ~~Print Just Listed Letters for the week~~
- Book haircut
- Call Adam regarding weekend bike ride

Chris works his way through the list, starting with the most important tasks first, printing his letters for the week. He moves on to following up the solicitor regarding the sale of Allerton Lane. Keeping a close eye on the time, he has 30 minutes before he needs to head off for his first buyer appointment. After another quick scan of the list, he books his haircut for Thursday and gives Sean a call regarding the November workshops.

- ~~Call Mary Robert regarding 37 Smith St, 0401 082 292~~
- ~~John returning your call about Albert St, 9871 2002~~
- ~~Roger from Williams Solicitors called regarding Allerton Settlement~~
- ~~Call Sean from real estate trainers about November Workshops~~
- Reading – How to increase your listings in ten easy steps
- Database training in September with Rosalie Graham
- ~~Pest and Building report 14 Nova Ave, Petersham~~
- ~~Print Just Sold letters for the week~~
- ~~Print Just Listed Letters for the week~~
- ~~Book haircut~~
- Call Adam regarding weekend bike ride

With ten minutes to go until his first appointment, Chris gathers his things and heads off for his buyer appointments. He is looking forward to getting out of the office, it is a beautiful day and he really enjoys meeting new buyers.

Thinking about Chapter 5

Although Chris was feeling good after his lunch break, he had a big morning and his energy levels are starting to fall. Having a list of tasks in his electronic diary, Chris didn't need to think too hard about what he needed to do. At a time when thinking starts to become more difficult, Chris knows he needs to move to tasks that he is familiar with or that don't require much effort, the opposite to prospecting. Doing his just sold and just listed letters, is just a matter of filling in a formatted template he uses each week. Just add the address, a couple of pictures and he's done. This requires very little thinking. Doing this in advance sets him up for the rest of the week. He has already put time aside in his diary to drop these letters around on Wednesday and Thursday. Having them done and out of the way, doesn't occupy any space for thinking and dramatically increases the chances of getting the letters delivered. Having the letters printed and ready to go, he won't have to do any thinking to get them out. He will just pick them up at the allocated timeslot and go. The less thinking he has to do around this task, the more likely it is to get done. The brain takes the easiest path, and if the letters are done and ready to do, it will get done. It also builds on his positive prospecting habits that he has developed. If Chris was to wait until he had time to do the letters, he would at best do them inconsistently, which would ultimately affect his business productivity.

Chapter 6 – 4:30pm–5:45pm

Chris returns to the office after a productive afternoon with buyers. He managed to get an offer on one house and good interest with a second inspection on another. He jumps on the phone and calls his owners with feedback and arranges a meeting to present his offer for tomorrow, blocking out a one-hour meeting with his owners between one o'clock and two o'clock on Tuesday. It is now almost five o'clock, so he again scans his emails. Two more enquiries have come in and a call from a mate. He moves them straight into his tasks list and shuts down his computer.

Chris has had a great day and, although feeling tired, he has achieved a lot. He spends a few minutes thinking about what he has achieved for the day. He is particularly pleased with the two new appraisals he generated from his morning calls and, although he didn't really enjoy making the cold calls, he is proud that he stuck it out and got through them without quitting. He also feels that he handled the problem with the building report well, and is confident he can get this one resolved soon.

Chris moves his attention to writing a list of things he wants to achieve tomorrow. His diary is already full with prospecting calls until twelve o'clock, however, there are a few other tasks he wants to follow up. He adds these to the list from today.

TASK LIST

- ~~Call Mary Robert regarding 37 Smith St, 0401 082 292~~
- ~~John returning your call about Albert St, 9871 2002~~
- ~~Roger from Williams Solicitors called regarding Allerton Settlement~~
- ~~Call Sean from real estate trainers about November Workshops~~
- Reading: How to increase your listings in ten easy steps
- Database training in September with Rosalie Graham
- ~~Pest and Building report 14 Nova Ave, Petersham~~
- ~~Print Just Sold letters for the week~~
- ~~Print Just Listed Letters for the week~~
- ~~Book haircut~~
- Call Adam regarding weekend bike ride
- Call John regarding his investment property
- Book car in for service
- Book restaurant for Friday night
- Go to council and get Greenway Rd contracts

Chris adds anything he can think of to the list for tomorrow, and blocks out time to get the tasks complete. There is nothing left to do, so he gathers up his things and heads home. It has been a productive day and he is completely worn out. He turns on the radio and enjoys some music along the way.

Arriving home, Chris dumps his things on the sideboard and heads into the bedroom to take a shower. Before jumping in, however, he gathers up his walking gear for the morning and lays it out in the wardrobe ready to go in the morning. He can now relax and unwind from his day. He is ready and looking forward to Tuesday and all the wins and challenges that are a part of being a high performing real estate agent.

Thinking about Chapter 6

As soon as Chris arrived back into the office, he knew he had to start planning the next day. The only thing left outstanding was to check to see what else had come in while he was out and either action them or delegate them to a task list. Doing this freed up his mind to think clearly about what he needed to do the next day. He was focused only on the things that were left undone. Doing this will allow his mind to rest and not hold any thinking after work. He put his thoughts into a safe place, his task list, then they could be forgotten.

He spent some time reflecting on his day and acknowledging what he had done well. This is important to building his positive habits that have made him a high performer. Even positive habits of high performers need to be acknowledged. The tasks that he finds difficult, such as cold calling, need particular attention. When performing tasks that we are resistant to, we need to constantly praise and acknowledge these habits. Every time we do, we strengthen the habits, making it a little easier each time. Should the task not result in any positive outcome, you still need to look for what went well. In Chris's case, he didn't generate any leads; however, he did acknowledge the fact that he stuck at it, knowing that, from time to time, he may not generate immediate business. He knows that if he persists, he will have wins, so the habit of completing the calls deserves to be acknowledged.

Having now dumped all his thoughts into his safe task list, and acknowledging what he had done well, he continued finishing the day with his brain in a toward mental state. This will stay with him through the night and he's much more likely to start the next day on a positive note.

Switching on the radio for his drive home helps rest his mind. Apart from thinking about driving home, although this doesn't require much effort because he does it every day, he can start to unwind and switch off his thoughts so he can relax and sleep well. Getting home, however, Chris knows he needs to get ready for the morning to ensure he gets up and goes for his walk. Getting his gear together and ready the day before increases his chances of getting this done. Chris has completed his day with a clear intention for the next. The brain likes safety and certainty and all the preparation Chris has done for the next day reduces any sense of anxiety and moves him into a toward state, ready to do it all again.

A final note

Even though the title 'A Perfect Day' suggests everything would have to go extremely well for the above scenario to take place, I'm a realist and understand that things sometimes just don't go well. The purpose of writing about Chris is to help you see areas in your day that you could improve upon, areas where you need to stop and areas that you are doing well in. It's not to suggest that having a perfect day, every day, is possible.

However, implementing the new learnings in the front part of the book will begin to put you on track to your perfect day. Remember, this book is not about quick fixes, or a single idea that will remarkably boom your career overnight. There are plenty of other books that claim to do that. Be patient and slowly implement new ideas over time. All new habits take time to adopt and nurture but, over time, the new high performance habits will dominate and then your career will be forever changed.

I would love to get your thoughts, ideas and feedback about the book. If you're interested in coaching for yourself or your team, I'd also love to hear from you.

You can find me at www.craighadfield.com.au or email me at craig@craighadfield.com.au

Craig Hadfield

Check out

Craig Hadfield coach, speaker, author.
www.craighadfield.com.au

Amanda Webb editor, for meeting all my deadlines.
www.amandawebbeditor.com

Kerrie Phipps coach, speaker, author. For support and assistance all the way though writing.
www.kerriephipps.com

References and recommended reading

David Allen, *Getting Things Done*

Jack Collis and Cyril Peupion, *Work Smarter Not Harder*

Jack Collis and Cyril Peupion, *Work Smarter: Live Better*

Dr Marshall Goldsmith, *The Success Delusion*

David Rock, *Your Brain at Work*

Dr Martin Seligman, *Learned Optimism*

Perry Zeus and Suzanne Skiffington, *Coaching at Work*

Perry Zeus and Suzanne Skiffington, *The Wisdom of Teams*

NOTES

NOTES

www.ingramcontent.com/pod-product-compliance
Lightning Source LLC
Chambersburg PA
CBHW051051230426
43666CB00012B/2648